What Others Are Saying . . .

I0866713

Todd Friel is a wealth of wonderful wisdom; an oasis of biblical truth in a desert of shallow theology. *Stressed Out* is drawn from a well that will refresh your soul.

Ray Comfort, CEO/Founder, LivingWaters.com

Todd Friel has done the Church a great service. Pastors, counselors, and church leaders will receive a great deal of help from this practical guide on some of the most debilitating issues in a believer's life. As our times become increasingly troubling and stressful, *Stressed Out* is a perfect antidote.

Pastor Emilio Ramos, Heritage Grace Community Church

The word "worry" is derived from the old English word "wyrgan." It means "to strangle." Worry harasses you and grabs you by the throat. Worry chokes. Todd properly analyzes the problem, lovingly identifies worry for what it is, then pushes your attention to the true solution. If you would like some biblical relief from the vice grips of the vice of worry, *Stressed Out* beats a straitjacket every time.

Mike Abendroth, Pastor of Bethlehem Bible Church
and host of *No Compromise Radio*

While depression and anxiety are sweeping the nation in epidemic proportions, there is hope to be found. Todd Friel has written a very biblical and accessible book to aid the weary sufferer. Drawing heavily from the Gospels, he is able to bring helpful prescriptions from the Lord Jesus — the Great Physician. *Stressed Out* is laced with Friel's unique brand of wit, along with his nurturing heart. This book is a great resource for the Church, and a joy to read.

Nate Pickowicz, Pastor of Harvest Bible Church

If you're currently struggling with the storms that rage in an anxious heart, this book offers concrete, authentic and wonderfully biblical help. Buy this book.

Pastor Lyndon Unger, writer at TheCripplegate.com

When Christians experience anxiety, we should acknowledge that we are not trusting in God and the teachings of His Word in the way that we should. When it happens, we should remember that God has the wisdom and power to overcome anxious thoughts, which in reality are an effect of the Fall (Genesis 3), and we can have victory in Him. Todd's new book offers hope as it helps you discover how to become conformed to the image of God's Son, including how your thinking can be transformed through the power of God's Word — starting with its very first verse.

Ken Ham, President/CEO, Answers in Genesis

Stressed Out is undoubtedly one of the most powerful, practical, and biblical books ever written on the subject of anxiety. I would even dare say that it's refreshingly revolutionary. You will breathe multiple sighs of relief as you read through its pages, and when you're done, you will delightfully find yourself reveling in an unspeakable joy that will give birth to a God-honoring calm in your heart, and exuberant worship in your life. Read it! Live it! Share it!"

Emeal ("E.Z.") Zwayne, President, Living Waters

As someone who has previously struggled through anxiety, I am very pleased that *Stressed Out* gently and surgically uses the soothing balm of Scripture to illustrate that the only appropriate remedy to this malady is to glorify God and enjoy Him forever. Unlike previous works on this subject, Mr. Friel has provided Christians laden with anxiety an indelible resource in recognizing and resting in the one true God and the eternal peace which comes only in His unwavering glorification.

Landon Chapman, owner/writer,
EntreatingFavor.com; host, FireAway! Podcast

Worry is one of the great obstacles that hinders our Christian effectiveness and service. *Stressed Out* not only helps us understand what anxiety is, but it also provides seasoned advice of how to deal with it from a biblical perspective. Straight-forward and direct, Todd Friel offers practical advice for those who deal with this debilitating enemy of life. Don't stress out, read this book!

Steven J. Lawson, President, OnePassion Ministries, Dallas, TX

Anxiety is a crippling emotion. People caught in the grip of gloom or struggling under the weight of worry naturally feel trapped and helpless. Christians contending with feelings of fear and melancholy often bear the twin burdens of guilt and shame as well. After all, Philippians 4:6 is one of the most familiar commands in the New Testament: "Be anxious for nothing."

But overcoming anxiety is not as simple as turning off a spigot. Those inclined to live by their natural feelings will simply succumb to brooding inactivity. There are solid biblical remedies for this malady, and they involve all the same means of grace that energize our sanctification. In this brilliant and wonderfully written book, Todd Friel clearly identifies and explains the biblical answers to the problem of anxiety. If you are frustrated in the quest for freedom from fear, or if you are trying to help someone who is afflicted with negative emotions, this book is just the right balance of encouragement, instruction, and biblical wisdom.

Phil Johnson, Executive Director, Grace to You Ministries

stressed OUT

A Practical,
Biblical Approach to Anxiety

Todd Friel

First printing: July 2016
Second printing: November 2017

Copyright © 2016 by Todd Friel. All rights reserved. No part of this book may be used or reproduced in any manner whatsoever without written permission of the publisher, except in the case of brief quotations in articles and reviews. For information write:

New Leaf Press, P.O. Box 726, Green Forest, AR 72638
New Leaf Press is a division of the New Leaf Publishing Group, Inc.

ISBN: 978-0-89221-743-4
Library of Congress Number: 2016941695

Cover by Diana Bogardus

Unless otherwise noted, Scripture quotations are from the New American Standard Bible (NASB), copyright © 1960, 1962, 1963, 1968, 1971, 1972, 1973, 1975, 1977, 1995 by The Lockman Foundation. Used by permission.

Scripture quotations designated NIV are from the New International Version®, copyright © 1973, 1978, 1984, 2011 by Biblica, Inc.™ Used by permission of Zondervan. All rights reserved worldwide.

Scripture quotations designated NKJV are from the New King James Version, copyright © 1982 by Thomas Nelson, Inc. Used by permission. All rights reserved.

Scripture quotations designated NLT are from the New Living Translation, copyright ©1996, 2004, 2007, 2013, 2015 by Tyndale House Foundation. Used by permission of Tyndale House Publishers, Inc., Carol Stream, Illinois 60188. All rights reserved.

Scripture quotations designated ESV are from the English Standard Version, copyright © 2001 by Crossway, a publishing ministry of Good News Publishers. Used by permission. All rights reserved.

Please consider requesting that a copy of this volume be purchased by your local library system.

Printed in the United States of America
Please visit our website for other great titles: www.newleafpress.com

For information regarding author interviews,
please contact the publicity department at (870) 438-5288.

New Leaf Press
A Division of New Leaf Publishing Group
www.newleafpress.com

Contents

Please note, this book is not attempting to offer medical advice. Before you make any decisions about beginning or eliminating any medication, you should consult your physician and your pastor to carefully make this decision.

Introduction

Start having hope right now. God is willing and able to fix your anxiety problem. He has done it for millions of people and He will do it for you too. You have His word on it. God is an anxiety expert. He has seen countless cases of "depression" and He would say to you, "Bring it on. I am ready, willing, and able to overcome your struggle."

Thankfully, God is not a physician with a crabby bedside manner; He delights in helping His children live an anxiety-free life. If you are willing to let your Great Physician diagnose and cure you, your anxiety will go away. You may have an occasional flare-up, but God can and will make you whole.

Jesus once asked a man who had been ill for almost four decades what seems like a peculiar question.

> A man was there who had been ill for thirty-eight years. When Jesus saw him lying there, and knew that he had already been a long time in that condition, He said to him, "**Do you wish to get well**?" (John 5:5–6).[1]

Why would Jesus ask what appears to be a no-brainer? Surprisingly, there are people who don't want to get well.

- Some people don't think they are ill.
- Some people like the attention that illness brings.
- Some people grow comfortable with their illness.
- Some people don't like to make the effort necessary to be healed.

May I ask you, "Do you wish to get well?" If you do, then God is prepared to help you live a truly abundant life (John 10:10). If you are willing to do

1. The Bible was not originally written on a computer. The inspired writers of the Bible had neither emoticons, italics, nor bold lettering. As you read the Bible verses contained in this book, you will notice that I have bolded words or thoughts to highlight them. Do not expect to see these in bold in your Bible.

some potentially uncomfortable self-examination and apply God's cure, then Jesus has a promise for you:

> If you continue in **My word**, then you are truly disciples of Mine; and you will know the truth, and the truth will **make you free** (John 8:31–32).

That is an offer we just shouldn't refuse! Is there a string attached? Yes, but it is not a chain with an anchor. You must be willing to "continue in His Word." You must find your diagnosis, prognosis, and cure in the Word of God. That means you must abandon other means that we often look to:

- Messages are not going to help you.
- Talk therapy is not going to help you.
- Sleeping pills are not going to help you.
- Coffee clutches are not going to help you.
- Thinking happy thoughts is not going to help you.
- Applying secular psychology is not going to help you.

None of these methods will remove your anxiety. God's methods will, and they are a lot cheaper than a day at the spa. If you are prepared to dive into His Word, submit to God and take His medicine, then Jesus will set you free from your anxiety.

Are you ready? Are you ready to be set free? Are you ready to understand why you feel the way you do? Are you ready to get to the root of your concerns? Are you ready to start thinking and feeling the way God designed you to? Are you ready to be changed in ways you can't imagine?

Section 1:

Understanding Anxiety

Chapter 1

Your Issue

If you go to a medical doctor with a sprained toe and tell him your elbow hurts, you will get a prescription, some exercises, and a nifty elbow brace, but your toe will not get the help it needs. The same thing is true for your emotions.

Emotions are tricky things and it is very easy to mislabel what you are feeling. No single word can accurately define an individual's emotions. Consider the nuances to the following words alone: anger, frustration, disappointment, irritation, resentment. These words are related, but each definition has a slightly different shade. That is what makes self-diagnosis so difficult.

Too often we self-diagnose our emotional issues and because we misdiagnose them, we never really heal. If you have wrestled with anxiety for a long time, most likely it is because you have not rightly understood the biblical explanation for anxiety.

If you start a journey headed in the wrong direction, you are not going to arrive at your destination. Even if you are off by an inch when you begin, you will be off by miles after a long journey and you will never get where you want to go.

How can we avoid making that mistake with anxiety? We must let the Great Physician examine us and make a biblical diagnosis. How does He do that? God examines and diagnoses us, and offers the cure through His Word.

> All Scripture is inspired by God and profitable for teaching, for reproof, for **correction**, for training in righteousness; so that the man of God may be adequate, **equipped** for every good work (2 Timothy 3:16–17).

How kind of God to provide us with a manual that has everything we need to live an anxiety-free life. We don't need the secular Diagnostic Statistical Manual that changes every few years. We need to trust the Word of God that never changes.

Best of all, when God examines us through His Word, there are no copays, no awkward conversations with a stranger, and we don't have to wear one of those dopey robes that tie in the back.

God will work with you privately and lovingly to apply His cure for your anxiety.

Organic Anxiety

Your wayward emotions can be neatly placed into one of two major categories: organic or non-organic.

Most likely, you are not suffering from organic depression. Even if the Diagnostic Statistical Manual categorizes your emotional challenge as clinical depression, you probably have nothing more than a common case of anxiety, which is very curable. But that doesn't mean we shouldn't take some time to make sure your issue is not chemical or physiological.

Diagnosing Organic Depression

Imagine walking into a doctor's office suffering from a stabbing pain in your back. You are sitting on a table covered with white paper when the doctor walks in and starts asking you questions. In fact, that is all he does; he only asks you questions. He doesn't examine you. He doesn't perform any blood tests. He orders no x-rays or MRIs. He merely inquires about your pain and then writes you a prescription. That doctor has not done his job. Doctors should examine a patient scientifically and then determine a diagnosis.

When it comes to diagnosing clinical depression, the scientific approach is thrown out the window because there is not a scientific method for determining depression. Depression is typically diagnosed based on presenting symptoms, which is the very opposite of the scientific deductive method.

Virtually every prescription written for depression is based on presenting symptoms without any scientific evaluation. That is why *The Journal of Clinical Psychology* recently revealed that 69 percent of antidepressant users never even met the DSM V criteria for major depressive disorder.

A psychology professor at Vanderbilt University who conducted extensive research on the effectiveness of antidepressants said, "I would say at least half the folks who are being treated with antidepressants aren't benefiting from the active pharmacological effects of the drugs themselves but from a placebo effect."[1]

Dr. Charles Hodges believes that less than 10 percent of depression diagnoses qualify as genuine organic illness. That should cause us to proceed with a great deal of caution before pursuing a medical solution to a non-medical problem.

There are some tests that can offer evidence of organic depression, but there are no conclusive scientific methods. Brain scans, along with hair, blood, and urinalysis tests can help determine if you have a physical issue that medicine might help. This testing is not nearly as sophisticated as we would like, but these should be considered before accepting a diagnosis of clinical depression.

There may be other physical reasons that can cause depression. Menstrual cycles, menopause, eating habits, lack of exercise or sunlight, alcohol consumption, low testosterone, weight issues, lack of REM sleep, vitamin deficiencies, or the side effects of other medications could be the source of your depressed emotions. These issues should also be addressed before you pursue a psychotropic prescription. The cure to your depressed mood may be as simple as getting more Vitamin D.

The Black Dog

Winston Churchill may or may not have been the originator of the phrase "a black dog howling" to describe depression, but it sure does describe the condition well. A black dog sits on the chest of its victim and howls unrelentingly.

When the black dog howls, the sufferer can hardly breathe, let alone spring out of bed and bound off to work. The black dog of depression is felt in the bones. The black dog knocks a person off his feet, onto his back, and takes him out of the game of life.

The black dog constantly nips at the heels of its prey. Dark thoughts echo in the brain. Thoughts of death come easily. A desire to escape society,

1. www.psychiatrist/com/jcp/article/Pages/2015/v76n01/v76n0106.aspx, http://www.apa.org/monitor/2012/06/prescribing.aspx.

family, and even life itself consume the thoughts of the quarry of the unleashed black dog.

The black dog that powerfully depresses one's emotions can even attack Christians. Charles Spurgeon, the Prince of Preachers, suffered from a sporadic form of devastating melancholy.

Being sad on occasion is not depression. Being worried about the future is not depression. Having a random dark thought is not depression. But a black dog may be a sign that you have a physiological condition that may be helped by medication.

Psychotropic drugs should be taken only with great wisdom, much research, and knowledge that these medicines are the least scientific of all medical prescriptions. The brain is staggeringly complex, and psychotropics are diagnosed like a dart game. Prescribing depression medicine is more of a guessing game than a science. Be very, very careful. Psychotropic medicine has many potentially severe side effects.

Having said that, if a Christian is hounded by the black dog, or is genuinely plagued with an organic issue (as best we can tell), medicine can be received as a blessing from God. Just because depression has been wildly over-diagnosed does not mean a Christian cannot avail himself of psychiatric medicine. Just make sure you receive wise medical and biblical counsel before you take any psychotropic medication.

NO SHAME

If any Christian shames you for requiring and utilizing psychotropic drugs, offer them grace and know that you are not sinning.

Your brain is an organ that can malfunction like any other organ. Born-again Christians can be assaulted by the black dog. Read that sentence again. Bible-believing Christians can experience debilitating depression and they should not feel ashamed, and they certainly should not feel like they are not saved.

Would you be embarrassed to tell someone you have high cholesterol? Would you be ashamed to reveal you have had your gallbladder removed? Then you should not blush if you have a genuine organic brain issue.

You are not your brain. Your brain is not what makes you, you. You are a spiritual being with a body. Your brain connects your spirit to the physical realm. Your brain processes, stores, reasons, and thinks, but your brain is not you. And just like any other organ, our brains can fail to function at normal levels. That is why you should not be ashamed if you experience organic depression.

Two Truths

If you do have a physiological reason for depression, there are two truths we would do well to consider. First, being diagnosed with organic depression does not mean we can blame our brains for our anxiety on the brain. A brain that is not functioning perfectly is not the cause of our anxiety; it simply reveals the anxiety that is already present in our members.

Did you catch that? Even if you have organic depression, you cannot excuse anxious emotions or behaviors because your brain is struggling. We cannot blame anxiety on our brains, but that does not mean we cannot recognize that some brains need help in functioning rightly so a person can overcome anxiety.

The second truth you must remember is that even after taking medication, you will still struggle with non-organic anxiety that needs to be addressed biblically. You will continue to experience anxious thoughts even after you receive the medication you need to bring your emotions under reasonable control. None of us escapes the malady of anxiety.

If you are one of the few people who actually has an organic issue that requires medication to get your thinking under control, you will still need to do battle with the problem that is common to all of us: non-organic anxiety.

Non-organic Anxiety

The second category of emotional issues is non-organic. This is where most of us find ourselves. Our brains are operating "normally," but we still have anxious or blue thoughts.

Non-organic anxiety is the issue that the overwhelming majority of us deal with every single day. This is the type of anxiety that this book seeks to address. Here are some synonyms that help us understand our focus. Do any of these words describe you?

- Worried
- Concerned
- Uneasy
- Fretful
- Nervous
- Apprehensive

Stressed Out

- Fearful
- Vexed
- Agitated
- Restless
- Upset
- Tense
- Miserable
- Blue
- Bothered
- Troubled
- On edge
- Irritable
- Panicky
- Sad
- Gloomy

Great news — if any (or all) of the words in that list describe you, then the Bible has much to say to you.

Do You Believe?

Do you believe that God has the power to get your anxious thoughts under control? Then you are in for an adventure. God will not necessarily remove every anxious thought from your mind, but He has the wisdom and strength to help you overcome and have victory over anxiety.

Your sanctifying God doesn't want to put a Band-Aid on your wound, He wants to flush it out and actually heal it. The process may sting a bit, but cleansing inevitably brings healing. Your Great Physician is prepared to diagnose you, give you a prescription, and not just heal you, but make you different. Better. Wiser. Stronger. Happier. Steadier. Healthier. Holier. More Christ-like. Are you ready to receive your diagnosis? Are you ready to receive a biblical prescription? Are you ready to apply the cure? If so, God is ready to change you in profound ways.

The Love of Christ! The Fullness, Freeness, and Immutability of the Savior's Grace Displayed!

James Smith

Believer, never *repine* at your trials, nor be over-anxious for their *removal.* They are *appointed* by Jesus as your *Purifier* — and are **choice blessings in disguise**!

Seek their sanctification, wrestle with God that you may see His love in every *stroke*, and look to Jesus that you may enjoy His presence when passing through the **flame!**

Nothing can hurt you — while Jesus is near you; and He is never nearer to you — than *when you are in the furnace!* For He sits right there as the *Refiner* . . . watching the process, regulating the heat, and waiting to effect a gracious deliverance — when the *ends* of His love are answered.

He is only preparing you for fresh manifestations of His glory — and fitting you for larger communications of His love.

In the furnace, you will *lose* nothing that is worth keeping — but you will *obtain* what is truly valuable![2]

2. James Smith, *The Love of Christ! The Fullness, Freeness, and Immutability of the Savior's Grace Displayed!* Originally published in 1860, emphasis in original, http://www.gracegems.org/2011/09/purge.html.

Chapter 2

Your Thinking

God wants to use your anxiety to do something magnificent in your life. Anxiety may not feel like a gift, but in a sense, it really is. It is an internal alarm that when activated should scream, "God wants to do something incredible for you."

Don't believe me? Consider the cricket!

> **The cricket**, in the spring, builds his house in the meadow, and chirps for joy because all is going so well with him. But when he hears the sound of the plough a few furrows off — then his sky begins to darken, and his young heart fails him!
>
> By-and-by the plough comes crunching along, turns his dwelling bottom-side up, and he goes rolling over and over, without a house and without a home! "Oh," he says, "the foundations of the world are breaking up, and everything is hastening to destruction!"
>
> But the gardener, as he walks behind the plough — does he think the foundations of the world are breaking up? No. He is thinking only of the harvest that is to follow in the wake of the plough; and the cricket, if it will but wait, will see the gardener's purpose.[1]

So what is God's purpose for your anxiety? The answer to that question begins in the Garden of Eden. At the pinnacle of God's creation, humans were made in the image and likeness of Almighty God (Genesis 1:27). We are God's image bearers, made to be His representatives to rule and subdue the earth (Genesis 1:28).

We were not made to be anxious. Humans were made to have steady, controlled, appropriate emotions, just like God. Humans were made to

1. A.B. Jack, "God's Providence," 1879, http://www.gracegems.org/2015/01/cricket.html.

mirror God and be a reflection of our Creator, who always has perfect emotions. You and I were originally built to think and feel the way God does, and we did, before the Fall. Our thinking was flawless and our emotions were perfect, but that all changed the day our great, great, great, great, great, great grandfather Adam decided to take a nosh of fruit.

When our federal representative Adam sinned, the whole world suffered the effects of the Fall, and our brains did not escape unscathed (Genesis 3:17). Because of the Fall, our brains feel the effects of the Fall. Theologians describe this as the "noetic affect of the fall."

> For the creation **was subjected** to futility, not willingly, but **because of Him** who subjected it, in hope that the creation itself also will **be set free** from its slavery to corruption into the freedom of the glory of the children of God. For we know that the **whole creation groans** and suffers the pains of childbirth together until now. And not only this, but also **we ourselves**, having the first fruits of the Spirit, even we ourselves groan within ourselves, **waiting eagerly** for our adoption as sons, the redemption of **our body** (Romans 8:20–23).

The world groans because of the Fall, and you and I do not escape its groaning (Romans 8:22). Because of the Fall, our logic is broken (Romans 1:23). Our reasoning is broken. Our thinking is broken. Our emotions are broken.

We are all in the same boat. Because of the Fall, you and I have brains that don't operate the way they should. That knowledge should give us the liberty to freely admit we have a problem. That knowledge should also give the Christian great hope, because Adam's sin and our Curse is not the end of the story.

The Bible tells us that God knew Adam would sin and we would suffer the effects of his decision (Acts 2:23). He did this in order to send His Son to redeem the world from the curse of sin.

> But God, being **rich in mercy**, because of His great love with which **He loved us**, even when we were **dead in our transgressions**, made us alive together with Christ (by grace you have been saved), and raised us up with Him, and seated us with Him in the heavenly places in Christ Jesus, **so that** in the ages to come He might show

> the surpassing riches of His grace in **kindness** toward us in Christ Jesus (Ephesians 2:4–7).

The Bible is a story of paradise lost and paradise regained.

- God created paradise for His image bearers to inhabit.
- His image bearers lost paradise when they sinned.
- Jesus Christ regained paradise by His death, burial, and Resurrection.
- On a day of His choosing, God is going to purge the world with fire and create a new heaven and a new earth where we will live with God in our eternal glorified bodies with perfectly functioning brains (1 Corinthians 15:42–44).

You and I are in the place of redemptive history where we anxiously await the redemption of our bodies.

> For the **anxious longing** of the creation waits eagerly for the revealing of the sons of God. For the creation was **subjected to futility**, not willingly, but **because of Him** who subjected it, in hope that the creation itself also will be **set free** from its slavery to corruption into the freedom of the **glory** of the children of God. For we know that the whole creation groans and suffers the pains of childbirth together until now. And not only this, but also we ourselves, having the first fruits of the Spirit, even **we ourselves groan** within ourselves, waiting eagerly for our adoption as sons, the **redemption of our body** (Romans 8:19–23).

The story of Jesus Christ is the greatest story ever told:

- Creation (God made everything to bring glory to Himself)
- Corruption (His creatures sinned against Him)
- Catastrophe (God destroyed the world with a Flood)
- Confusion (The Tower of Babel caused God to disperse people)
- Christ (God sent His Son to redeem rebellious people)
- Cross (Jesus received the punishment sinners deserve)
- Consummation (At the end of time, God will recreate everything perfectly)

You and I are living between the Cross and Consummation. Christians eagerly await the consummation of all things, when everything (including us) will function the way they did before the Fall. But God does not wait until Judgment Day to start fixing us.

When God saves us, He not only forgives us of our sins (a one-time act), but He begins the process of sanctifying our thinking (an ongoing act). In other words, God goes about the business of fixing your brain so you think, act, and feel more like Him. That is why your anxiety has purpose.

Our gracious God wants to restore you to the way an image bearer should be, and He wants to use your anxiety to do that. Your anxiety should scream at you, "You need help with your thinking." God's response to your cries is, "I am ready, willing, and able to fix you." God wants to progressively heal and fix your brain so you think and feel correctly, the way He does. God is going to glorify you and permanently fix your emotions for eternity, but He does not wait until you die. God wants to start fixing your thinking now. God stands ready to steady your emotions starting today.

Would you stop and ponder that for a moment? God loves you so much that He wants to be a part of your life and restore you to the way we were before the Fall. He wants to turn you into the image bearer you are (Colossians 3:10). This brings us great joy and it brings God great glory. Our ancestors used to rejoice in this knowledge.

Puritan Thomas Watson said, "God's afflicting rod is a pencil to draw Christ's image more distinctly on us. Affliction is God's flail to thresh off the husks, not to consume the precious grain."[2]

God loves to take our struggles and transform them into trophies of victory that He places on His mantle of praise. Paul understood that perfectly even as he underwent a physical malady that just wouldn't go away.

> And He has said to me, "My grace is sufficient for you, for power is **perfected in weakness**." Most gladly, therefore, I will rather boast about my weaknesses, so that the **power of Christ** may dwell in me. Therefore I am well content with weaknesses, with insults, with distresses, with persecutions, with difficulties, for Christ's sake; for when I am **weak**, then I am **strong** (2 Corinthians 12:9–10).

God loves to take your weaknesses and turn them into testimonies of His strength working in you. When you are weak (which you are), then He is strong (which He is). This is all a part of God's plan.

---

2. http://www.gracegems.org/2014/03/affliction.html.

You are not an oddity or a solo struggler. You are a broken image bearer whom God wants to restore for His name's sake. You should not be ashamed to admit that you struggle with anxiety, because all of God's fallen image bearers do.

The Effects of the Gospel

When Jesus Christ died on the Cross, He shed His blood for the forgiveness of your sins. If you have repented and placed your faith in the Lord Jesus Christ, all of your sins — past, present, and future — are nailed to that tree (Colossians 2:14). That is the gospel, no more and no less.

Strictly defined, the gospel is this: Jesus died for sinners. But the effects of the gospel are far reaching. The effects of the work of Jesus on the Cross include:

- We are declared innocent (Colossians 1:14).
- We are brought near to God (Ephesians 2:13).
- We are adopted into God's family (Romans 8:14–17).
- We have peace with God (Colossians 1:20).
- We have everlasting life (John 3:16).
- We have a cleansed conscience (Hebrews 9:14).
- We can live an abundant life (John 10:10).
- We are made heirs with Christ (Romans 8:17).
- We have an inheritance (1 Peter 1:3–4).
- We are made saints (Romans 1:7).

One of the amazing effects of the gospel is sanctification (Hebrews 13:20–21). God makes us progressively more holy. God is willing to give you more and more power to overcome your anxiety. God delights in fixing His broken children.

What Is Anxiety?

This is where God's examination of your heart might be a bit painful. When it comes to biblically defining anxiety, there is some good news and there is some great news. It is not going to feel like that initially, but hang in there, this is very, very good news indeed.

Let's begin with the good news: if you are worried about anything, then you are sinning! You read that right. Because God commands us to not be anxious about anything (Philippians 4:6), then we are sinning when we are anxious.

That is very good news, because every time God commands us to not sin, He always provides a way for us to overcome that sin. Always. That means you have hope. That means you don't have to be worried anymore. That means you can have victory over anxiety.

The world likes to file all of our issues in a cabinet marked "Disease." Non-organic anxiety is not a disease. If you, like the rest of us, wrestle with anxiety, you do not have an illness. You have a garden-variety case of . . . sin. You don't need a prescription; you need sanctification. The great news is that God is an expert in sanctification, and He is not a begrudging helper. He delights in sanctifying us.

It stings a bit to realize that all of our anxious thoughts are actually sinful thoughts, but this should not leave us in a ditch of devastation. If we only think about how sinful we are (and we are), then we will land in a pit of despair. While we must grasp that our anxiety is actually a violation of a command of God, we must also grasp that God has a remedy for the sin that ails us.

This might be the most difficult part of your healing process — admitting that you do not have an illness, you have a sin problem. My friend, do not let that crush you. Remember, God never commands us to do something without providing the means for us to be obedient. Jesus commands you to not be anxious and, true to form, He provides you with 12 anxiety relievers to help you not sin by being anxious.

These are not principles to simply help you get through the day without biting your nails. These are God's ordained means for making us more like His Son. Jesus gives us 12 anxiety relievers to change us and to make us look the way we were made to look.

> For though we walk in the flesh, we do not war according to the flesh. For the weapons of our warfare are not carnal but mighty in God for pulling down strongholds, casting down arguments and every high thing that exalts itself against the knowledge of God, **bringing every thought into captivity** to the **obedience of Christ** (2 Corinthians 10:3–5; NKJV).

God wants to do more than make us feel better most of the time; God wants us to think and act like Jesus. God wants to take our broken sinful frames and fix them to make us like Himself. This brings Him great glory and it should bring us great joy.

Consider the nobility of this. God's "psychiatry" far transcends all man-made systems designed to help us cope. Your Creator is prepared to radically reprogram your brain so you think the way God Himself thinks.

Prepare to see the caring hand of God as He provides you with the means to overcome your sinful anxiety and change you from "glory unto glory" (2 Corinthians 3:18).

Prepare to live the joy-filled life He wants you to live (John 10:10). This abundant life can be yours. You can leave your anxious thoughts behind. You can sleep soundly. You can rise in the morning without a black cloud hanging over your head. More than that, you can be restored to your original design: a glorious image bearer of the God of the universe.

Your God cares for you (1 Peter 5:6–7). Your God does not want you to be anxious. Your God wants to help you. Your God wants to relieve you of your burdens. Your God wants to make you better beyond your wildest imaginings.

Consider the wheat:

> A few ears of wheat were growing in the corner of a field, and it was promised to this wheat that it would one day be brought before the Queen. But by-and-by the *mower* came with his sharp scythe and cut the wheat, and feeling the sharpness of the scythe, it said, "I shall never stand before the Queen!"
>
> Presently it was laid in the wagon, and pressed and borne down by the other sheaves, and again arose the cry of distress and despair. But, more than this, it was laid on the threshing-floor, and the heavy *flail* came down upon it.
>
> It was taken to the *mill*, and cut and cut and cut; then it was kneaded into bread; and at last it was placed in the *hot burning oven*. Again and again was heard the cry of utter, hopeless despair. But at length the promise was fulfilled, and the bread was placed on the Queen's table!
>
> There is a great spiritual truth beneath the fable. Christians are *God's wheat*, sprung from the incorruptible seed of His Word, and from the precious seed of the crucified, buried body of our Lord

— and He purposes that one day they shall stand before Him! But there needs *much preparation*.

There comes the sharp scythe of *bereavement* — the loss of child or parent or spouse.

There comes the oppressive burden of care.

There comes the *severe tribulation,* seasons of adversity and disappointment.

There comes *the mill*, the trial that utterly breaks us down, and fills the whole spirit with distress.

There comes the hot furnace of agonizing pain or fear.

All these are doing their appointed work, stirring up faith and prayer, humbling to the very dust — and yet lifting up the Christian, by leading him nearer to God, and enabling him at length to say, *"It is good for me that I have been afflicted!"*[3]

Not Alone

You are not in this alone. God does not simply toss you a "How to not be anxious" manual, then abandon you to figure this out by yourself. You have a Savior who is prepared to take you by the hand and begin walking you down the path of victory over the sin of anxiety.

Your Savior is not going to grab you by the hand and drag you to where you need to go. Jesus is a sympathetic high priest who wants to help you overcome your fears, your frailties, and your sinful emotions.

> Therefore, since we have a **great high priest** who has passed through the heavens, Jesus the Son of God, let us hold fast our confession. For we do not have a high priest who cannot **sympathize with our weaknesses**, but One who **has been tempted** in all things as we are, yet without sin. Therefore let us **draw near with confidence** to the throne of grace, so that we may receive mercy and **find grace** to help in time of need (Hebrews 4:14–16).

The devil tempted Jesus in the wilderness. The disciples tempted Jesus to be annoyed because of their faithless questions. Jesus' own half-brothers tempted Jesus to be depressed because of their lack of faith in Him. You have a sympathetic high priest.

3. George Everard, "The Home of Bethany," 1873, http://www.gracegems.org/2016/02/allegory.html.

Jesus knew He was going to receive the wrath of His Father for sinners who hate Him. Can you imagine the temptation for Jesus to run? Jesus knows what it means to be tempted. In other words, Jesus gets you.

- Are you afraid of something? Jesus understands.
- Are you worried about the future? Jesus understands.
- Are you concerned about the opinion of others? Jesus understands.

Jesus was tempted beyond anything that you and I will ever face; yet He didn't sin. You have a God who understands you.

Jesus Christ is ready to aid you in your grand transformation from anxious sinner to God-glorifying image bearer. Can you admit that your anxiety has been nothing more and nothing less than sin? If you can, you are now ready to begin the battle of mortifying your sin of anxiety.

Perhaps you have been worrying for years. Perhaps you are exhausted from constantly fretting about the future. Perhaps you have conveniently catalogued your anxiety into a file labeled "typical emotional issues." It is time to label that file correctly.

- Let's call your anxiety what it is: a noetic effect of the Fall.
- Let's call your anxiety what it is: sin.
- Let's call your anxiety what it is: an opportunity to not be anxious and become more like Jesus Christ.

If we do not submit to the Word and agree with God that our anxiety is a sin, then we will not be helped. God resists the proud, but He offers grace to the humble (James 4:7). May I invite you to humble yourself with the millions of people who have also confessed that it is a sin to be anxious? If you do not, then I am afraid that God is going to "resist you." But, if you will humble yourself, God will stoop to help you and then He will exalt you in due time (James 4:10).

This is the first step to being radically transformed by the One who loves you more than anyone in the universe. While this is most certainly humbling, this should also fill us with great joy. We do not have to be anxious anymore; God will fix us.

Instead of being sinfully anxious, that news should make you anxious with anticipation. Your sympathetic high priest is ready to transform your mind. Are you ready to be transformed?

The Great Sympathizer!

David Harsha

"Jesus wept!" (John 11:35) The Son of God, the Creator of the universe, the Lord of glory — *in tears!* Amazing sight!

How plainly do those tears show the tenderness of Jesus! And how animating to think that the heart of Jesus now that He reigns in glory — is still full of sympathy and full of love for His suffering disciples in this *valley of tears!*

Weeping believer, you whose tears are flowing — come to Jesus for sympathy, and tell Him all your grief.

He has words of comfort for you — precious promises.

He can console you as none else can.

He is the same in all ages — the same yesterday, today, and forever. The eye that dropped its tears at the tomb of Lazarus — will be fixed upon you in all the scenes of anguish through which you may be called to pass before reaching the bright world of everlasting joy.

Remember that He who is now seated on the throne of heaven, radiant in celestial glory — was once afflicted on earth, that He might know how to sympathize with you in the hour of your unutterable anguish.

Oh, rejoice that you have so sympathizing a Friend, who is ready to relieve your grief, and to conduct you to those happy mansions, where God shall wipe away all tears from your eyes.

Who can tell how great is the sympathy of the Son of God, who came from the bosom of the Father — from the unapproachable splendor of heaven — to bear our infirmities, to lighten our burdens, to wipe the tears from our eyes, and to turn our sorrows into everlasting joys?

Always view Jesus as the great Sympathizer of His disciples — and in the time of your keenest anguish, look to Him for compassion and relief. He will regard your cries of misery. Yes, He whose heart felt and bled for sinners, will speak soothingly to you, and give you a foretaste of Heaven, even in a world of tribulation.

Oh, the ineffable compassion of our blessed Redeemer![4]

4. David Harsha (1827–1895), "The Savior's Ministry," http://www.gracegems.org/2015/08/sympathizer.html.

Chapter 3

Your Anxiety

Not every "anxious" thought is sinful! Some anxiety is sinful and some anxiety is not, and it would be tragic to apply a sin-elixir to non-sinful anxiety. It would be a double tragedy to suggest that you should never have an emotion when trouble comes knocking. God does not intend for us to be emotionless drones. Let me explain.

There are two kinds of biblical anxiety; one type is sinful, the other is not. Jesus' 12 anxiety relievers should be applied only to the sinful variety of anxiety, but not to non-sinful anxiety. Therefore, we need to determine which kind of anxiety is sinful, and what kind is not. Jesus Himself provides us with the perfect example for knowing which emotions are sinful, and which emotions are not.

When Jesus arrived at the funeral of His beloved friend, Lazarus, He saw several things (John 11:1–46):

- Grief
- Weeping
- Hopelessness
- Death
- Confusion
- The effects of sin

When Jesus heard the wailing of the mourners, the Bible says that Jesus was troubled:

> When Jesus therefore saw her weeping, and the Jews who came with her also weeping, He was **deeply moved** in spirit and was **troubled** (John 11:33).

The Greek language tells us that Jesus literally "troubled Himself." In other words, the circumstances didn't produce Jesus' emotions; Jesus exhibited the correct emotions based on the situation. Do you hear the difference?

Jesus was not powerless in His response to tragedy. He demonstrated that He was totally in control of His feelings and He thoughtfully responded to the point of weeping (John 11:35). Events did not control Jesus' emotions. Jesus controlled and displayed His emotions properly in response to events. Jesus' emotions were not passive; Jesus' emotions were under His control.

Now fast forward to John 14:1. Jesus was eating His final meal with His disciples before His crucifixion. He was preparing them for His departure and He knew they would be anxious. Jesus commanded them, "Do not let your heart be **troubled**."

Uh oh. John 11 tells us that Jesus was troubled. But two chapters later, Jesus commanded the disciples to not be troubled. That should cause us to put the brakes on and ask, "Is it OK to be troubled (John 11:33) or is it a sin to be **troubled** (John 14:1)?"

The word "troubled" is usually interpreted "anxiety," and because the same word (troubled) is used in both cases, we can conclude there is a good kind of troubled/anxiety (the kind Jesus had), and there is a sinful kind of troubling/anxiety (the kind you and I tend to have). What's the difference?

1. It is OK to mourn when a loved one dies.
2. It is OK to cry when a tragedy happens.
3. It is OK to enter into someone else's grief.
4. It is OK to be troubled over the effects of sin.
5. It is OK to be sad when we experience something tragic.

We are not emotionless automatons. We are humans who have God-designed feelings and it is perfectly normal to express our emotions if they are not sinfully motivated.

> There is an appointed time for everything. And there is a time for every event under heaven. . . . A **time to weep** and a time to laugh; a **time to mourn** and a time to dance (Ecclesiastes 3:1–4).

Non-sinful sadness is a part of the human experience. It is not necessarily a sin to have a blue feeling. If your emotions are responding to tragedy, death, disaster, hardship, or the effects of the Fall, then it is perfectly normal to feel sad.

It is extraordinarily easy for appropriate feelings to quickly turn into sinful emotions. As soon as our sadness spills over into fear, worry, concern, nervousness, anxiety, or tension, then we are no longer in control of our God-given emotions. The goal of sanctification is for us to control our feelings and not be controlled by our feelings.

God's emotions are stable, predetermined, and under control. God is not like a pubescent teenager who careens from one emotion to another. God's emotions are always exactly right all the time. God never loses it. God is never stressed. God does not get frustrated. That is how we are supposed to feel.

Jesus was not troubled by His emotions; Jesus troubled Himself. Jesus controlled His emotions; His emotions did not control Him. Jesus led His emotions; His emotions did not lead Him. He responded rightly with the right sentiment at the right time. He did not freak out. He was not fearful. He was not concerned about the future. Jesus reacted with sadness to a sad event. That is good news for us; if Jesus felt sad, that means we can too.

You and I can be sad in appropriate situations, but we cannot be afraid or worried about the future. We can weep, mourn, and feel unhappy, but we cannot fret, bite our nails, obsess, fear, and cause ourselves to have restless nights because we are worried about the future. Fearful anxiety is precisely the type of worrying that Jesus told the disciples, and by extension us, to not have.

- Be sad that you lost a beloved family member, but do not curse God.
- Be sad that your child receives a low SAT score, but do not fear for his future.
- Be sad that you received a devastating test result from your doctor, but do not fear for your life.

Not every sad emotion is sinful. Sadness, disappointment, and grief are a part of the human experience. You and I can have controlled emotions that are perfectly human responses to grievous situations, but we are commanded to not be:

- Worried
- Concerned
- Uneasy
- Fearful
- Vexed
- Agitated
- Restless
- Fretful
- Nervous
- Apprehensive
- Bothered
- Troubled
- On edge
- Irritable

Stressed Out

- Upset
- Tense
- Miserable
- Depressed
- Panicky
- Sad
- Gloomy

The Diagnostic Statistical Manual does not allow for grieving a loss; the Bible gives us permission to mourn. If you have experienced a disappointment or tragedy, take your time and grieve. While it is possible that prolonged mourning might need to be addressed, as a rule you should not let people rush you through the grieving process. Just make sure you are troubling yourself and not being troubled by sinful anxiety.

Being Anxious Vs. Being a Good Steward

Can we ever worry about financial issues? Can we be concerned about the future of our children? Can we be nervous about a move or job transfer? No. To fret over the future is to sin (Matthew 6:25). But that does not mean we cannot be aware of bad or challenging events that can happen in the future and wisely prepare for them. We just can't be anxious about "what ifs."

- It is fine to prepare for your child's education. It is not fine to be vexed about it.
- It is fine to plan a vacation. It is not fine to freak out if your flight gets cancelled.
- It is fine to consult with doctors and plan your medical care. It is not fine to fear dying.
- It is fine to strategize about selling your home. It is not fine to panic about it not selling.
- It is fine to plan for your financial future. It is not fine to be anxious about your finances.
- It is fine to imagine getting married and living happily ever after. It is not fine to lose sleep over finding Prince Charming or Princess Buttercup.

There is a fine line between sinful anxiety and planning for the future. We can and should prepare for the future; we just can't sin as we do so. To be sure, there is much that can cause anxiety these days, but Christians are called to fear not (Luke 12:23).

- We are commanded to not be anxious about the future (John 14:1).
- We are called to have our emotions under control (Galatians 5:22–23).
- We are warned that anxiety about the future is an insult to God (Matthew 5:25–39).

While we might be comforted by the fact that every human being on earth has committed the sin of anxiety, that does not let us off the hook. We are accountable for our emotions. Fear of the future is common, but it is not acceptable.

That is why you must be aware of which feeling you are actually having. If you are sad because of sin, death, or disaster, that is fine. If you are sad because you are worried about tomorrow, that is not fine.

Remember the Line

There is a fine line between sinful emotions and non-sinful emotions. This is not only true regarding anxiety, but with many other emotions:

- A Christian can have righteous anger at evil, but a Christian cannot be sinfully angry because a child spills milk.
- A Christian can laugh at wholesome humor, but a Christian cannot sinfully laugh at bawdy jokes.
- A Christian can have joy when someone gets saved, but a Christian cannot have joy when someone gets hurt.

God-given emotions can be enjoyed rightly or abused sinfully. It is up to us to make sure we act like God by having the right emotion at the right time for the right reason. And know this, when you cross the line into sinfully anxious, then God has already forgiven you and He stands ready to help you grow and not think like that again. Why? Because you have a sympathetic high priest who wants to fix your thinking so you can have the same joy that He has (John 15:11).

Consideration

James Buchanan, 1840

The general end of affliction is the moral and spiritual improvement of believers — in other words, their progressive sanctification, and their preparation for glory. Oh! how important must the right use of affliction be, if it is intended to terminate in such a blessed result. It stands connected with our everlasting welfare — with all that we can enjoy on earth, and all that we hope for in Heaven.

But more particularly, the day of adversity is intended for our INSTRUCTION. The *Lord's rod* has a voice which speaks to us lessons of heavenly wisdom. Therefore, we are required "to *hear the rod,* and Him who has appointed it."[1]

1. http://www.gracegems.org/2015/10/rod.html.

Chapter 4

Your God

The most important thought you think is what you think when you think about God. So may I ask, "What do you think about when you think about God?" How you answer that question can and will drive your emotions.

If you think God is distant, angry, scary, unloving, capricious, disinterested, or weak, it is very easy to be anxious. But if you think God is kind, warmhearted, tender, loving, good, and caring, then you can have peace when chaos is all around you.

Do you think God is for you, or is God against you? Is God your friend, or is God your opponent? Is God pleased with you, or is God angry at you?

How you answer those questions is crucial as you begin the process of dealing with your anxiety. Knowing God's attitude toward you will determine the course of your success or failure in managing your emotions.

Is God for You?

God is either for you or He is against you. God isn't sort of for you or kind of against you. God is either totally for you or totally against you; and you do not get to decide which one it is. God's attitude toward you is not based on your performance or His whimsy. God's attitude toward you is based on your position.

If you are **not** in Christ, God is **not** for you. If you have not repented of your sins and placed your faith in the Lord Jesus Christ, your Maker is your enemy. Your Creator is your foe. God is your worst nightmare.

Because you continue to rebel against your sovereign God in thought, word, and deed, you have set yourself squarely against your King. More than that, you are amassing for yourself a cup of wrath. At a time of God's own choosing, He will pour out that never-ending cup on you for eternity.

If you are not hidden in Christ, God is decidedly against you, and frankly, you should not be anxious, you should be terrified. You should not just lie awake at night, you should pace the floors. You should have no rest. No peace. No joy. No hope.

Money issues, work issues, and family issues are the least of your concerns. You, a guilty criminal, are going to face the furious wrath of God on the Day of Judgment. If you have not been forgiven of your sins, then your biggest problem has not been solved. God is your enemy and you are His foe. God Himself has His face set against you.

On the Other Hand

If you are in Christ, then your biggest problem has been solved: all of your sins have been forgiven. If you are in Christ, then you have been adopted into the family of God. If you are in Christ, then God is no longer against you; He is for you.

If you have turned from your sins and trusted Jesus Christ, you are no longer God's foe, you are His friend. If you are a Christian, you have been plucked out of Adam and placed into the Lord Jesus Christ. That means God loves you with the same love that He has for His own Son.

- God's face is not set against you.
- God is not conspiring to harm you.
- God is not simmering at 211 degrees just waiting to boil over on you.

If you are a Christian, God is for you. The Creator and Sustainer of the universe is actually totally and completely for you. Because you are in Christ, God is on your side. He desires your best. He wants only good things for you. He will never, ever do anything evil to you.

Knowing and believing that God is for you is a crucial truth in the battle to overcome anxiety. You must be persuaded by Scripture that this is true or the rest of this book will be a waste of time for you.

Here are 13 verses from Romans 8 to persuade you that God is for you.

Proof #1

Would you like to know what the third person in the Trinity is doing right now? He is praying for you. That's right — the Holy Spirit of God is interceding on your behalf at this very minute.

> In the same way the Spirit also **helps** our weakness; for we do not know how to pray as we should, but the Spirit Himself **intercedes for us** with groanings too deep for words; and He who searches the hearts knows what the mind of the Spirit is, because He **intercedes for the saints** according to the will of God (Romans 8:26–27).

Did you notice that the Holy Spirit is praying FOR you? He is not praying against you; the Holy Spirit only petitions God for your best.

As you read these words, the Holy Spirit of God is talking to the Father about you. He is not asking God to make your day a mess. He is not begging the Father to toss a calamity your way. He is praying only for the best to happen for you.

Knowing that the Holy Spirit is praying for your best raises a question: what is best for you?

You and I have a tendency to think that financial stability, good health, and a secure future are what is best for us. In other words, we tend to focus on external things. While those things are important, the Holy Spirit wants something more for you.

The Holy Spirit wants to give you internal things. The Holy Spirit wants you to possess attributes the world cannot give. The Holy Spirit wants you to have the fruit of the Spirit: love, joy, peace, patience, kindness, goodness, faithfulness, gentleness, and self-control (Galatians 5:22–23).

Because God is more interested in our internal character than our external comforts, He is willing to do anything FOR us in order to grow us. God loves you so much that He is even willing to bring pain into your life to cultivate fruit of the Spirit.

Proof #2

You might think your life is a mess right now, but God doesn't.

> And we know that God causes all things to work together **for good** to those who love God, to those who are called according to His purpose. For those whom He foreknew, He also predestined to **become conformed to the image of His Son**, so that He would be the firstborn among many brethren; and these whom He predestined, He also called; and these whom He called, He also justified; and these whom He justified, He also glorified (Romans 8:28–30).

The world wants one thing for you; God wants another.

- The world offers you finer wine; God wants you to act like His Son.
- The world offers you a bigger house; God wants you to think like His Son.
- The world offers you a fancier wardrobe; God wants you to be clothed in the righteousness of His Son.

The world offers things that are relatively easy to obtain. God offers you profound things that require more effort than online shopping. The world wants you to conform to its image. God wants you to be transformed to think and act the way human beings were created to act: like image bearers of Almighty God. To accomplish this, He is causing all things to work together for your good.

Proof #3

Romans 8:31 is definitely a clobber verse that proves God is for you.

> What then shall we say to these things? If **God is for us**, who is against us (Romans 8:31)?

It couldn't be clearer than that! And just in case you need proof, Romans 8 gives you all the evidence you need to know that God is for you.

> He who **did not spare** His own Son, but delivered Him over **for us** all, how will He not also with Him **freely give us** all things? Who will bring a charge against God's elect? God is the one who justifies; who is the one who condemns? Christ Jesus is He who died, yes, rather who was raised, who is at the right hand of God, who also **intercedes for us** (Romans 8:32–34).

The best proof you can have that God is for you is the gospel of Jesus Christ. You can know that God is for you because His own Son volunteered to embark on a rescue mission to save you from the consequences of your sin.

Proof #4

God is so for you that He died for you so that you could be forgiven, justified, and saved from the wrath that is to come. And just to put some icing on top of the cake, Romans 8 concludes:

> Who will separate us from the love of Christ? Will tribulation, or distress, or persecution, or famine, or nakedness, or peril, or sword? Just as it is written,
>
> "For Your sake we are being put to death all day long;
> We were considered as sheep to be slaughtered."
>
> But in all these things we **overwhelmingly conquer** through Him who **loved us**. For I am convinced that neither death, nor life, nor angels, nor principalities, nor things present, nor things to come, nor powers, nor height, nor depth, nor any other created thing, will be able to separate us from **the love of God**, which is **in Christ Jesus** our Lord (Romans 8:35–39).

God is so FOR you that nothing can separate you from His love. The devil can't, you can't, your parents can't, your behavior can't, your anxiety can't, your boss can't, your mother-in-law can't, bad health can't, a calamity can't, and your feelings can't. Nothing can separate you from God's love if you are in Christ Jesus.

Even when you go through hard times (which you will), God is FOR you and you will overwhelmingly conquer.

- Knowing that God is so FOR you that He died FOR you, can you trust Him to ordain your circumstances to grow you in profound ways?
- Knowing that God loves you so much He sent His Son to receive His wrath on your behalf, can you trust Him to design what is best for you, even if it is hard?
- Knowing that God is more interested in your holiness than He is in your happiness, can you trust that everything He puts you through is for that lofty purpose?

Being fully persuaded that God is FOR you must be the foundation for dealing with your anxiety. If you think that God might occasionally be against you, it is certain that you will wobble when hard things happen. But when you know that everything happens **for** you, then your thinking will rightly process the events in your life and you will conclude, "It is well with my soul."

Our sights are set on comfort; God's goal for us is Christ. If we each had our way, we would all be gazillionaires; God wants us to be rich in character.

We desire happiness, but God's desire for us is holiness. God does not give us the life we dream of; God gives us the life we need in order to be conformed to the image of His Son, Jesus Christ.

> Therefore, having been justified by faith, we have **peace with God** through our Lord Jesus Christ, through whom also we have obtained our introduction by faith into this grace in which we stand; and we exult in hope of the glory of God. And not only this, but we also **exult in our tribulations**, knowing that **tribulation brings about** perseverance; and perseverance, proven character; and proven character, hope; and hope does not disappoint, because the love of God has been poured out within our hearts through the Holy Spirit who was given to us (Romans 5:1–5).

You and I have some really ugly rough spots; God loves us so much He is willing to apply some sandpaper to slough off those rough patches. That truth should cause our painful experiences to be turned to joy.

> **Consider it all joy**, my brethren, when you encounter various trials, knowing that the testing of your faith **produces** endurance. And let endurance have its **perfect result**, so that you may be perfect and complete, lacking in nothing (James 1:2–4).

God sees your sinful weaknesses and gives you the strength to overcome them. God will even do something hard for you in order to slough off those rough spots. Difficult circumstances should not cause us to be anxious, they should cause us to trust God more.

> Before I was afflicted I went astray,
> But now I keep Your word.
> You are good and do good;
> Teach me Your statutes. . . .
> It is **good for me** that I was afflicted,
> That I may **learn Your statutes**. . . .
> I know, O LORD, THAT YOUR JUDGMENTS ARE RIGHTEOUS,
> AND THAT IN FAITHFULNESS **You have afflicted me**.
> O may Your loving-kindness comfort me,
> According to Your word to Your servant (Psalm 119:67–76).

If you are anxious, you need to believe this: God wants to use your anxiety to teach you, change you, and grow you. If you do not see your negative circumstances as an opportunity to grow, you won't. And brace yourself for this: God loves you so much, He will up the ante until He causes you to break and look only to Him for your rescue.

- God can and will do whatever it takes to pry the idol out of our hands.
- God can and will do whatever it takes until all of your hope is put in Him and Him alone.
- God can and will do whatever is necessary to help you realize that you don't run the universe.
- God can and will do whatever is needed to move you from being a self-centered, self-absorbed sinner to a God-reliant, God glorifying, fully trusting, humble follower of Jesus Christ.

You have a choice — you can let God break you, or you can humble yourself (James 4:7). Either way, He is going to have His way with you . . . in a good way. Why not let your loving Father teach you how to grow out of your sinful anxiety? Why not humble yourself instead of feeling the weight of God's heavy hand? You can choose, but as you do, know that God's preference is to gently lead and guide you toward holiness.

God Wants to Grow You, Not Crush You

Here is the scene: Jesus Christ is eating His last supper with the disciples. He is on the way to His execution. Undoubtedly, you and I would be anxious for what was about to happen, but not Jesus.

Kind, considerate, thoughtful, loving Jesus knew the disciples were about to face difficult circumstances upon His crucifixion. He knew they would be inclined to worry once their rabbi had been murdered. Instead of being anxious for Himself, Jesus preoccupied Himself with the anxiety of His disciples for the next three chapters (John 14:1, 18, 25, 27–29, 15:26, 16:5–7, 17–19, 22, 28, 32–33).

Facing the most horrific pain any man has ever known, Jesus spends three uninterrupted chapters in the Gospel of John focusing on one subject only: 12 anxiety relievers for the disciples and, by extension, us. That is how kind, thoughtful, and loving your Savior is. He did not worry about Himself.

He lovingly gave His last lengthy discourse so you and I don't have to worry.

Should you be inclined to think the disciples' worries pale in comparison to yours, consider. See if this list looks familiar.

- **Health and safety:** The Pharisees had often conspired to arrest Jesus and have Him killed. It is safe to say that the disciples had to wonder, "Will they come after us once they take Jesus out of the way?"
- **Careers:** The disciples had left their businesses to follow Rabbi Jesus. If Jesus died, then they would no longer have the means to support themselves and they couldn't return to a job they had walked away from.
- **Family:** No doubt the disciples were warned by family and friends to not follow a Galilean rabbi. Do you suppose the disciples wondered what Thanksgiving was going to be like when they returned home because their teacher had been found guilty of blasphemy and publicly crucified in ignominy?
- **Fear of man:** Not only would family make fun of the disciples for following a man who claimed to be God, but so might everyone else in Israel.

Our worries are no different than the worries of the disciples. Do you worry about:

- Death
- Your career
- Your finances
- Your child's future
- Your child's spouse
- Passing a test
- Getting pregnant
- Keeping your spouse
- Your future
- Your family
- Your retirement
- Your child's career
- Your home
- Finding a spouse
- Not getting pregnant
- Having a sin discovered

Your struggles may be slightly more 21st century, but they are no different than the worries the disciples had. That is why Jesus' words to the disciples are so practical and helpful for us. Their worries are your worries. Their concerns are your concerns. Their cure for anxiety is your cure for anxiety.

There are very real issues we face, but Jesus commands us to not have anxiety. And remember, when Jesus commands us to not sin, He always provides a means for us to not sin. When it comes to anxiety, Jesus doesn't provide one means for us to not sin, He provides 12.

How kind is Jesus? How caring is Jesus? How compassionate is Jesus? Jesus was facing mutilation, mockery, and murder, yet He focused on the fears of His followers. If you have ever wondered if God cares about you and your troubles, this scene should forever remove that doubt.

- See your Savior marching to the Cross to receive the wrath of God on your behalf, yet He focused His last extended teaching on your emotions.
- See your Savior willingly stagger as a sheep to the slaughter, yet He concerns Himself with you.
- See your Savior approach His execution, but instead of being anxious for Himself, He concerned Himself with your anxiety.

Jesus Christ cares so much about your emotions that He lovingly prescribed 12 anxiety relievers during His final Passover dinner and even as He walked to the Garden of Gethsemane where the treacherous disciple with clean feet would betray him.

There are three clear lessons from this:

1. Jesus cares about you and wants to help you live a worry-free life.
2. Jesus practiced what He preached. If anyone should have been worried, it was Jesus; yet He showed no signs of anxiety while He marched to the Cross.
3. Anxiety must be a big issue or Jesus would not have spent His last moments with the disciples teaching them how to overcome it.

Knowing that Jesus felt more pressure to be anxious than you ever will should make you confident He understands your issues. Knowing that Jesus never committed the sin of anxiety should give you hope. He knows what He is doing. Knowing that Jesus cares enough about you to provide 12 anxiety relievers while He was walking to His execution should comfort you. Prepare now to see the 12 anxiety relievers that your kind, wise, heavenly Friend has provided for you.

All Things Working for Good

Dr. Octavius Winslow

It is palpably clear and emphatically true that all that occurs in the Lord's government of His people **conspires for**, and works out, and results in, their highest happiness, their **greatest good**.

The gloomiest and most painful circumstances in the history of the child of God, **without a solitary exception**, are all conspiring, and all working together, **for** his real and permanent good.

The painful and inexplicable events, which at the present moment may be thickening and deepening around your path, are but so many problems in God's government, which He is working out to their **certain, satisfactory, and happy results**.

All things under the government of an infinitely great, all wise, righteous, and **beneficent Lord God**, work together **for good**. What that good may be, the shape it may assume, the complexion it may wear, the end to which it may be subservient, we cannot tell. **To our dim view it may appear an evil**, but to God's far seeing eye it is a **positive good**.

Oh, truth most divine! Oh, words most consolatory!

Beloved of God, all these things are **for you**! Do not be afraid!

Will it not be a good, if your present adversity results in . . . the dethronement of some worshiped idol; in the endearing of Christ to your soul; in the closer conformity of your mind to God's image; in the purification of your heart; in your more thorough fitness for heaven?

Will it not be a real good if it ends with: a revival of God's work within you; a stirring you up to more prayer; in enlarging your heart to all that love the same Savior; in stimulating you to increased activity . . . for the conversion of sinners, for the spreading of the truth, and for the glory of God?

Oh yes! good, real good, permanent good must result from all the Divine events in your history.

In a little while; oh, how soon! You shall pass away from earth to heaven, and in its clearer, calmer light you shall read the truth, often read with tears before, "And we know that God causes everything to work together **for the good** of those who love God and are called according to His purpose **for them**."[1]

1. Excerpts from http://www.gracegems.org/2002/Romans%208-28.htm, emphasis added.

Section 2:

12 Anxiety Relievers

Chapter 5

Anxiety Reliever #1: You Have a Diagnosis

Your anxious friend calls you seeking advice. He is worried about his finances, family, career, and the future of America. What would you recommend?

- Hire a great money manager
- Find a really good family counselor
- Read *The 7 Habits of Highly Effective People*
- Buy some land in Montana and stock plenty of food and water

While that advice may seem sensible, Jesus did not offer any "practical advice" to His disciples who were certain to be troubled when their Rabbi and Savior left them. Instead, He launches into a three-chapter diatribe on anxiety. He begins by diagnosing their problem.

> Do not let your heart be troubled, **believe in God**, believe also in Me (John 14:1).

Talk about unexpected. The announcement of Jesus' departure could give anyone a nervous breakdown, but instead of offering practical advice, Jesus does what any good doctor would do: He diagnosed the disciples' anxiety problem. His conclusion: when we are anxious, it is because we are not believing right.

Jesus is telling you that our anxiety is a faith issue. When we are worried, we are not trusting God the way we should.

Please note, Jesus did not say you are not a believer when you are anxious, He said you are merely acting like an unbeliever. Jesus did not say that you are not saved, but He made it clear that you are acting like you are not.

Your Great Physician has diagnosed your anxiety problem as a faith problem. In the moment that you are anxious, you are lacking the right kind of faith.

If you believe that your omnipotent God is for you and nothing can befall you that is not from His beneficent hand, then you would not be anxious. When you are worried, you are simply not trusting your God.

This is not the only time that Jesus diagnosed anxiety as a faith issue. Jesus regularly taught that anxiety is rooted in a lack of faith in God.

1. Sermon on the Mount

Jesus told the crowds not to worry about their lives, food, water, or clothing.

> For this reason I say to you, **do not be worried** about your life, as to what you will **eat** or what you will **drink**; nor for your body, as to what you will **put on**. Is not life more than food, and the body more than clothing (Matthew 6:25)?

Jesus commands us to not be anxious about the basic necessities of life. Therefore, if we worry about food, water, and clothing, then we were sinning. Hold on — it gets worse. If it is a sin to worry about life-sustaining necessities, how much more sinful is it to worry about more trivial matters like vacations, being tardy, having lumpy gravy at Thanksgiving, running out of gas, oversleeping, not having clean socks?

Jesus then diagnoses this kind of anxiety as a faith issue:

> **You of little faith!** Do not worry then, saying, "What will we eat?" or "What will we drink?" or "What will we wear for clothing?" For the Gentiles eagerly seek all these things; for your **heavenly Father** knows that you need all these things (Matthew 6:30–32).

Ouch. Jesus ties our anxiety issue directly to our faith and His critique is stinging. In essence, Jesus asked, "Have you forgotten that God is fully aware of your needs? Have you forgotten that you are more precious to your Heavenly Father than the birds of the air and the lilies of the field" (Matthew 6:26–30)?

Pagans worry about the bare necessities; Christians should not. Unbelievers worry; believers have a Heavenly Father who loves us and knows our needs better than we do.

2. Sinking Faith

After preaching that anxiety is a faith issue, Jesus demonstrates that anxiety is a matter of trust.

> When He got into the boat, His disciples followed Him. And behold, there arose a great storm on the sea, so that the boat was being covered with the waves; but **Jesus Himself was asleep** (Matthew 8:23–24).

Clearly Jesus was not anxious about the storm; but the disciples were.

> And they came to Him and woke Him, saying, "Save us, Lord; we are perishing!" He said to them, "Why are you **afraid**, you **men of little faith**" (Matthew 8:25–26)?

Jesus' message is clear: "If you are anxious, you have a faith problem." When you and I are scared to death of death, Jesus makes it clear that we are men and women of little faith. Why? Because we have forgotten that God has ordained our birth date and our death date:

> Your eyes have seen my unformed substance; and in Your book were all written the **days that were ordained for me**, when as yet there was not one of them (Psalm 139:16).

God is the One who keeps us alive (Colossians 1:17). God is also the One who determines our death date. If God wants you alive today, you will live. If God wants you dead today, you will die.

If you have a fear of flying, you can rest assured that if God wants you in heaven, He will end your life on the ground as easily as in the air. Conversely, if God wants you alive, you can go zip-lining on a piece of dental floss and you will not die. That's what the author of Psalm 139 said.

> Where can I go from Your Spirit?
> Or where can I flee from Your presence?
> If I ascend to heaven, You are there;
> If I make my bed in Sheol, behold, You are there.
> If I take the wings of the dawn,
> If I dwell in the remotest part of the sea,
> Even there **Your hand will lead me**,

> And Your right hand **will lay hold of me**.
> If I say, "Surely the darkness will overwhelm me,
> And the light around me will be night,"
> Even the darkness is not dark to You,
> And the night is as bright as the day.
> Darkness and light are alike to You (Psalm 139:7–12).

If you could choose the date of your death, what day would you choose? Unless it happens to be the day that God has chosen for you, it will not be the right day. God, who knows you better than you know yourself, has selected the absolute best day for each of us to die.

If you have an appointment with an oncologist because there is a shadow on your x-ray, you will be anxious if you are lacking faith in the author of life and death. If you remember that your days are in His hands, then you will not fear what the doctor might say.

Should we tempt God by living recklessly? No, but we can face danger confident that God has pre-ordained whether we are going to die or not. When you fail to remember that, then you are bound to be anxious in the face of death.

3. More Sinking Faith

If you lack faith in God and worry about your life, you are not alone. Just six chapters after the first time Peter sank like a stone, he and the rest of the disciples exhibited a lack of faith that resulted in anxiety.

> Immediately He made the disciples get into the boat and go ahead of Him to the other side, while He sent the crowds away. After He had sent the crowds away, He went up on the mountain by Himself to pray; and when it was evening, He was there alone. But the boat was already a long distance from the land, **battered by the waves**; for the wind was contrary. And in the fourth watch of the night He came to them, walking on the sea. When the disciples saw Him walking on the sea, they were **terrified**, and said, "It is a ghost!" And they cried out **in fear**. But immediately Jesus spoke to them, saying, "Take courage, it is I; **do not be afraid**."
>
> Peter said to Him, "Lord, if it is You, command me to come to You on the water." And He said, "Come!" And Peter got out of the

> boat, and walked on the water and came toward Jesus. But seeing the wind, **he became frightened**, and beginning to sink, he cried out, "Lord, save me!" (Matthew 14:22–30).

If we don't pause to appreciate the kindness of Jesus in this moment, we will miss an opportunity to see the epitome of patience. Most of us would yell, "How many times do I have to tell you? Don't worry!" Instead, we see Jesus do two things: rescue Peter and remind him that his problem is an issue of faith.

> Immediately Jesus stretched out His hand and took hold of him, and said to him, "**You of little faith, why did you doubt**?" (Matthew 14:31).

Jesus, the patient teacher, reminds Peter again that fear and worry are matters of faith. When you and I fear death, we exhibit the same kind of small faith that Peter had.

Fearing for our lives must be very common or Matthew would not have repeated two nautical faith lessons in one book. The bad news: just because fearing for our lives is common does not make it any less sinful.

When you fear for your life, you are not trusting God. Remember that the next time you find a lump or a bump. Your benevolent Father has already ordained your days and you will not die one day before you are supposed to.

4. Feeding Thousands

In Matthew 14, Jesus miraculously fed 5,000 men, plus women and children. In Matthew 15, Jesus fed 4,000 men, plus women and children. In Matthew 16, the disciples were confronted with a large, hungry crowd and they appear to have a case of amnesia.

> And the disciples came to the other side of the sea, but they had forgotten to bring any bread. And Jesus said to them, "Watch out and beware of the leaven of the Pharisees and Sadducees." They began to discuss this among themselves, saying, "He said that because we did not bring any bread." But Jesus, aware of this, said, "**You men of little faith**, why do you discuss among yourselves that you have no bread? Do you **not yet understand or remember** the five loaves of the five thousand, and how many baskets full you picked up? Or the

seven loaves of the four thousand, and how many large baskets full you picked up (Matthew 16:5–10)?

How quickly the disciples, and we, forget God's miraculous provision for us. Day after day He provides our daily bread, but on the only day our cupboards are bare, we fret. O we of little faith.

TWO TYPES OF LITTLE FAITH

There are two types of little faith that produce anxiety. We can have a little faith in a big object, or we can have a big faith in a little object.

The first type of little faith is when we have little faith in our big God. That is the type of little faith Jesus was talking about in the Sermon on the Mount, the two sinking stories, and the bread amnesia of Matthew 16. When you and I have anxiety, the first thing we should examine is our faith in God. If it is robust, we will not worry. If our faith in God is little, we will be anxious.

The second type of little faith we can have is a big faith in a small object: ourselves. When you and I think we are the ones responsible for an outcome, we are in essence placing our hope in ourselves. No wonder we have anxiety; we are trusting a puny object: us.

Jesus describes that type of little faith to the disciples who were given a special gift to perform signs and wonders. When they failed to cast out a demon in Matthew 17, Jesus diagnosed their problem as a misplaced faith issue.

> When they came to the crowd, a man came up to Jesus, falling on his knees before Him and saying, "Lord, have mercy on my son, for he is a lunatic and is very ill; for he often falls into the fire and often into the water. I brought him to Your disciples, and **they could not cure him**." And Jesus answered and said, "**You unbelieving and perverted generation**, how long shall I be with you? How long shall I put up with you? Bring him here to Me." And Jesus rebuked him, and the demon came out of him, and the boy was cured at once.
>
> Then the disciples came to Jesus privately and said, "Why could we not drive it out?" And He said to them, "Because of the **littleness of your faith**; for truly I say to you, if you have **faith the size of a mustard seed**, you will say to this mountain, 'Move from here

> to there,' and it will move; and nothing will be impossible to you" (Matthew 17:14–20).

Jesus was not telling the disciples they had a small faith in God, because He told them if they had a mustard-sized faith in God, they could perform miracles. Jesus was teaching the disciples they had a little faith because they were placing their faith in themselves. The disciples were guilty of the same thing you and I are frequently guilty of: placing much faith in ourselves instead of God.

In most cases of anxiety, we are practicing both types of little faith. We forget that God is sovereignly controlling every single molecule in the universe, so we think we need to pick up the slack. The process typically works like this:

- We do not constantly remind ourselves of God's promises.
- We forget that God is in control.
- We think we need to take matters into our own hands.
- We plan, plot, scheme, and imagine each and every potential outcome.

That is when we start experiencing insomnia. We twist and turn, imagine and re-imagine, and never feel peace. When we think God is either too busy, disinterested, or too weak to care, we place our faith in a frighteningly feeble object: ourselves. This is a double slap to the face of God:

1. When we have a little faith in God, we are in essence saying, "You can't handle this."
2. When we have a big faith in ourselves, we are in essence saying, "I can handle this better than God."

Determining the reason for this is the first thing we need to do in order to make a faith adjustment.

The Culprit

It is safe to say that virtually every presenting sin is not our actual problem. Most sins are merely the fruit of a much more rotten root. The root of our sin of anxiety is pride and idolatry. This is how it works.

- We fail to read, study, and ponder God's Word.
- Something challenging, hard, or scary happens.

- We forget that God is sovereignly controlling every detail of our lives.
- We panic.
- We forget God.
- Our fleshly pride determines that we need to deal with the situation.
- We think, plan, plot, and strategize every scenario.
- We effectively play God. We are the idol of our own universe.
- We remain anxious because we realize that many things are out of our control and we can't really guarantee the outcome of anything.

Pride and idolatry are at the root of virtually every sin, but no sin exemplifies that more than the sin of anxiety. Anxiety says, "Excuse me, God, but I think You are in my seat." When anxiety kicks in, we are placing our faith in:

- Our wit
- Our looks
- Our money
- Our cunning
- Our education
- Our connections
- Our skills
- Our plans
- Our wisdom
- Our pedigree
- Our intelligence

Consider how offensive that is to God when He commands us to:

> Trust in the Lord with all your heart
> And do not lean on your own understanding.
> In all your ways **acknowledge Him**,
> And He will make your paths straight (Proverbs 3:5–6).

When we fail to heed this command, we demonstrate we have little faith in Him because we are the idol of our own lives. And that is when big anxiety kicks in.

Anxiety says, "I've got this. I am trusting myself."

God says, "I've got this. Trust me."

When you submit to God and allow Him to reign in your life, you cannot descend into anxiety. Here is how that works:

- You read, study, and ponder God's Word.
- Your Bible teaches you to do what you can do to address the situation but trust God for the outcome.

- Something challenging, hard or scary happens.
- You remember that God is sovereignly controlling every single detail of your life.
- You are calm in the storm.
- The storm rages harder and you begin to worry, but you remind yourself that there is no need to be anxious because your King has all things under His sovereign control.
- You are acting like the obedient servant whom God loves as He reigns in your life.
- You have peace knowing that God works all things for your good and His glory.

Perhaps you think this is too simple. Well, perhaps you have simply made your anxiety issue more complex than it needs to be.

Perhaps you have read books that have told you that anxiety is the result of stinkin' thinkin.' Those books are wrong. Jesus taught that anxiety is not primarily a thinking issue — it is first and foremost a faith issue. Anxiety means you are worshiping you when *you* should be trusting in *the Lord.*

Your Brain Is Like a Train

Think of your brain as being like a train. Secular psychiatrists (and far too many Christian counselors) tell us that our thinking leads our train. Their train lines up like this:

- The engine is your brain: your thinking leads your actions and emotions.
- The second car in your brain train is decisions based on your thinking.
- The caboose is the emotions that are produced by your decisions.

Secular books are called "self-help books" because you have to help yourself by fixing your thinking. If you can just think right, then you will feel right. God is nowhere to be found in this model.

Jesus orders your emotions differently. Jesus makes faith the engine of your thinking.

- You place your faith in something/someone.
- Your thinking is based on the teachings of that something or someone.

- You make decisions based on what you have learned.
- Your emotions follow your thinking and decisions.

You do not merely think thoughts, you think thoughts and have emotions based on what you believe. Faith is the foundation on which everything else builds. What you believe and how much you believe it is the key to victorious Christian living.

So how do we get more faith in God? This may sound like circular reasoning, but it is not. You will gain more faith in God by increasing your knowledge of God.

> So **faith comes from hearing**, and hearing by the Word of Christ (Romans 10:17).

If you had a friend who was genuinely rich but always worried about his finances, it would not be enough to soothe him by constantly saying, "Don't worry." It would be far more helpful to show him his bank balance, financial statements, and investment reports. This knowledge of the truth would increase your friend's confidence in his situation. The same thing is true with our faith in God; learning facts about God in the Bible increases our faith and confidence in Him.

This is why you should actually be excited about your anxiety. Your anxiety should be an alarm bell that rings, "It's time to trust your God." Every time you are anxious, instead of being worried, you should think, "I get to increase my faith in God." That is precisely what God wants to do with your anxiety.

God wants to do something far more profound for you than take your worries away or make you a better theologian. God wants to decrease your anxiety by increasing your faith.

Jesus wants to tear down your idols. Jesus wants to dethrone you and sit squarely on the throne of your life as you trust Him to work all things for your good. Here is the great news — He is ready, willing, able, and very worthy.

How exciting is that? God wants to actively get involved with your emotions and turn chaos into confidence. God wants to move you from being self-centered to being God-focused. God wants to take your fallen, broken, sinful, busted thinking that leads to sleepless nights and fearful days, and give you a glorious hope for the future.

When we reign in our lives, the results are anxiety, heartbreak, disappointment, and fear of the future. When Jesus reigns, the results are peace, joy, contentment, hope, and even courage.

There is no better test of your faith in God than tribulations. If your response to struggles has been anxiety, then you have been demonstrating little faith. In fact, you have been wasting your troubles. God has designed them for you to grow in faith and Christlikeness.

God wants to use your anxiety to grow your faith. Don't waste your anxiety!

You have already made a great start by picking up this book. You have admitted that you have an anxiety problem. You have now discovered that you have a faith problem. Do not despair — God does not want to leave you where you are; He wants to grow you, change you, fix you. God wants to make you better by increasing your faith in Him.

The Cure

Jesus doesn't diagnose sinful anxiety as a faith issue in John 14:1 and then move along to a discourse on end times or good stewardship. Instead, He spends the next three chapters of John providing your cure. Each of the following 11 anxiety relievers is designed to increase your faith and conform you into the likeness of your Savior (2 Peter 2:4) by increasing your knowledge of Him.

Increased knowledge of God will increase your faith, which will improve your thinking and emotions. Your increased faith will change your thinking, which will drive your actions, which will lead to anxiety-free emotions.

Each one of the anxiety relievers Jesus offers is not a mystical formula that brings a magical sense of calm in the storm. Christianity is not a mystical religion; Christianity is a thinking religion grounded in truth and believed by faith. When you believe right, then you will study what is right, think what is right, and your emotions will be right.

> And do not be conformed to this world, but be transformed by the **renewing of your mind**, so that you may prove what the will of God is, that which is good and acceptable and perfect (Romans 12:2).

Mastering your emotions requires growing your faith and mastering your thinking. When you firmly believe that Jesus' words truly relieve your anxiety, then you will do what He tells you to do.

Your sympathetic High Priest is not going to scold you. Jesus will not call you names or shame you. Instead, your loving Savior gently sets before you the means to grow in faith that leads to joyful living.

Jesus is willing to go to work on your anxiety problem by growing your faith in Him without shame, guilt, or scolding. Are you ready to respond? Are you ready to be obedient to His command to "believe in God, believe also in Me" (John 14:1)? If you are, then He is ready to change you, grow you, and give you peace.

The Remedy for a Troubled Heart!

James Smith

We often trouble ourselves. We often allow our hearts to be tossed about like the waves of the sea, without any real cause. Our Savior forbids it. He forbids it in tender love. He forbids it because it is injurious. Inward commotion, or confusion unfits us for social duties, pious exercises, and usefulness in the church of God. It lays us open to temptations, and fosters unbelief and anxiety. Our Lord would have us calm, patient, and composed; therefore He says, "Let not your heart be troubled!"

He prescribes a *remedy for heart trouble*, or inward anxiety:

1. "Believe in God." Believe in God as your Father — as loving you, acting for you, and rejoicing in your welfare.

See Him ordering all events with consummate wisdom; over-ruling all with infinite skill; and sanctifying all to your welfare, by His sovereign grace.

There is no room for "chance" — for His government is perfect.

There can be no unkindness — for His love is infinite.

All will be directed right — for He personally superintends every detail in the universe! The floating of the atom, the rolling of the sea, and all the movements of every mind — are alike under His control and direction!

2. "Believe also in Me." Believe:

that I sympathize with you;

that I feel the deepest interest in your welfare;

that I never withdraw My eye or heart from you for one moment;

that I will support you in every place, and under every trial;

that My arm shall be stretched out for you, to lean upon,

as you come up out of the wilderness of this world;
that I will save you to the uttermost;
that I will show you a brother's love;
that I will stand by you as a firm friend in every distress;
that I will overturn all the designs of your foes!

Believe that I will fill My characters in your experience, as your Savior, Brother, Friend!

Believe that I will fulfill My word to you; every promise, the largest, the kindest — "for Heaven and earth shall pass away — but My word shall not pass away, until all be fulfilled."

"Let not your heart therefore be troubled. It does not befit you as My redeemed child. It is injurious to you. It dishonors Me. It can do no good. Therefore watch against it, as against a foe! Pray against it, that you may have grace to overcome it. Strive against it, for it is your duty. Always view worry as an evil, as an evil which it is possible to overcome.

View it as inconsistent with your profession, as injurious to your soul, as dishonoring to your God."

There is no *cause* for you to be troubled, for your God performs all things for you. It is inconsistent for you to be troubled, for your Savior has bequeathed you His peace. It is sinful for you to be troubled, for you are bidden to cast all your care upon the Lord, and are assured that He cares for you.

All your worry will not change the color of a hair, will not weaken the power of one foe, will not lighten a single burden — it is therefore *folly* — as well as *sin!*

The remedy is before you. It was prescribed by the great Physician; it has proved effectual in innumerable instances; it is just suited to you, it was intended for you! Will you use it, and prove its beneficial effect?

Remember Jesus, that Jesus who:
lived for you,
labored for you,
suffered for you,
died for you,
rose for you, and
is now in Heaven *pleading* for you.

He says, "Let not your heart be troubled. You believe in God — believe also in Me!"[1]

1. http://gracegems.org/Smith5/remedy_for_a_troubled_heart.htm.

Chapter 6

Anxiety Reliever #2: You Have a Future

Somebody started a rumor: "If you are too heavenly minded, you will be of no earthly good." That person needs to be tracked down and informed that Jesus' second anxiety reliever teaches the exact opposite of that sentiment.

> In My Father's house are many dwelling places; if it were not so, I would have told you; for I go to **prepare a place for you**. If I go and prepare a place for you, I will come again and **receive you to Myself**, that where I am, **there you may be also** (John 14:2–3).

If you are worried about what is happening in the here and now, Jesus tells you to turn your thoughts to the hereafter.

- When you are worried about the temporal, think about the eternal.
- When you are worried about the fleeting, think about the forever.
- When you are worried about the physical, think about the ethereal.

What were you thinking about the last time you were anxious? If you are honest, you would have to admit you probably weren't imagining the glories of heaven.

Undoubtedly, you don't worry about what is going to happen in heaven, but you worry about what is going to happen on earth. Jesus explains why.

> Do not store up for yourselves **treasures on earth**, where moth and rust destroy, and where thieves break in and steal. But store up for yourselves **treasures in heaven**, where neither moth nor rust

destroys, and where thieves do not break in or steal; for where your treasure is, there **your heart will be also** (Matthew 6:19–21).

If you are worried about earthly matters, it is because your heart is invested in this planet. God doesn't want you to love the things of this world (1 John 2:15), He wants you to look forward to the things you are going to experience in heaven, chiefly, Him.

> Their destiny is destruction, their god is their stomach, and their glory is in their shame. Their mind is set on earthly things. But **our citizenship is in heaven**. And we **eagerly await a Savior** from there, the Lord Jesus Christ (Philippians 3:19–20; NIV).

If you want to worry less, Jesus tells you to think about heaven more.

- When people let you down, think about spending eternity with the One who never disappoints.
- When sin is dragging you down, look up to heaven and ponder spending eternity with the One who is going to abolish sin for all time.
- When you find yourself in the pit of despair, let the Morning Star shine brightly by remembering that you will never feel despondent when you enter your eternal home.

Jesus is not suggesting you never think about earthly issues. We are commanded to be good stewards of our time, talents, and resources, but we are also commanded to not place our hope in earthly things, which will one day be fuel for a massive Judgment Day fire.

> But the day of the Lord will come like a thief, in which the heavens will pass away with a roar and the elements will be destroyed with intense heat, and the **earth and its works will be burned up**.
>
> Since all these things are to be **destroyed** in this way, what sort of people ought you to be in holy conduct and godliness, looking for and hastening the coming of the day of God, because of which the heavens will be **destroyed by burning**, and the elements will melt with **intense heat**! But according to His promise we are **looking for new heavens** and a new earth, in which righteousness dwells (2 Peter 3:10–13).

The next time you are inclined to worry about something physical (home, car, furniture, clothing), just remember it is all going to be kindling when God purges this sinful world with fire and creates a new heaven and a new earth.

Consider how much time, effort, and emotional energy went into your earthly treasures. Some day soon they will be worth nothing. Ashes don't sell for much. Earthly things are here for you to enjoy, not worship. When you worry about temporal issues, that is a clear indicator that you are worshiping that which is only meant to be enjoyed.

Does this mean we trash everything we own? No. We are not Gnostics who believe that all material things are evil.

God created a very good creation for us to use and enjoy. He also made the creation for us to be masters over it and not vice versa. When you have anxiety, the creation is mastering you. To reverse the roles and keep your priorities straight without descending into Gnosticism or monasticism, Jesus commands you to think about heaven.

Long-term Gratification

You and I love instant gratification. Jesus implores us to stop being shortsighted and focus on forever. The things of this world are not insignificant, but they are not nearly as meaningful as eternal things.

You and I fret about food, clothing, reputation, careers, education, and a million temporal things because our hearts are set on them. If our hearts were set on heavenly things, we would not be worried about earthly frivolities like health, sustenance, and security.

- When earth hammers away at you, ponder what is in store for you.
- When people wound you, ponder Jesus drying your tears (Revelation 21:4).
- When circumstances disappoint you, ponder the joys of eternity.

How do we do that? Let's work through some typical concerns we have and re-orient our thinking from earthly minded to heavenly minded.

Shelter

Do any of these scenarios sound familiar?

- Your real estate agent helps you find the home of your dreams. Multiple parties make an offer and you wait anxiously to learn if your bid wins.
- You get transferred and you travel to your new town to purchase a home. You have 48 hours to purchase a home for you and your family. You worry you won't find one in time.
- You live in an apartment, but you hear about a foreclosed home that you could afford. You anxiously wait for the bank to qualify you.

Listen again to the words of Jesus, "I go to prepare a place for you."

Jesus, the Lord who made heaven and earth, is preparing a customized dwelling for you in heaven. He is not subcontracting out this job or hiring a construction crew. Jesus Christ Himself is building a place for you.

When Jesus calls you home, you won't have to stand in the lobby. You won't have to show a license and give a credit card for incidentals. You won't end up in a smoking room with double beds when you reserved a non-smoking king. Your room will be ready and it will be perfect.

Here is the kicker — it will not be the dwelling that makes you happy, it will be the One with whom you get to live. You will get to dwell in the mansion of God with God. You are going to be given a room in the house of the King with the King. No outer court for you. No guesthouse for you. You get to dwell in the big house with the Master who actually desires your presence. God doesn't need anything or anyone, and yet He wants you to be with Him forever in His mansion (John 14:3). Ponder that the next time you are stressed out about your dream home.

Food

Worrying about food is easy. We can stress about dinner plans, having the right ingredients, or getting a table at a restaurant on Saturday night. Maybe you have panicked about the meal you had to prepare for your in-laws at Christmas. Perhaps you are concerned about the catering at your wedding reception. Maybe your food issues are far less glamorous because you simply don't know how you are going to pay for next week's groceries. Whatever your food anxiety is, you need to ponder this.

In Luke 12, Jesus exhorted the disciples to live an alert life, prepared for the return of their Master. And then He made a statement that undoubtedly staggered the disciples.

> Blessed are those slaves whom the master will find on the alert when he comes; truly I say to you, that **he will gird himself to serve,** and have them **recline at the table**, and will come up and **wait on them** (Luke 12:37).

Whoa! Jesus Christ is not only preparing a home for us, but you and I are going to get to partake of the wedding feast of the Lamb (Revelation 19:6); and the waiter at this feast is going to be Jesus Christ Himself.

God's Son is going to serve you a meal in heaven. The King is going to serve the rebels. The Perfect One is going to serve the sinners. The owner is going to serve the debtors. Your God is going to once again humble Himself for your sake.

This is not the first time we see Jesus humbly serving His servants a meal. King Jesus prepared breakfast for the disciples after He rose from the dead.

> So when they got out on the land, they saw a charcoal **fire already laid** and fish placed on it, and bread. Jesus said to them, "Bring some of the fish which you have now caught."
>
> Jesus said to them, "Come and have breakfast." None of the disciples ventured to question Him, "Who are You?" knowing that it was the Lord. Jesus came and took the bread and **gave it to them**, and the fish likewise (John 21:9–13).

And if that isn't humble enough for you, in John 13:4–17, we see the Master wash the feet of His disciples after dinner. That's right, God washed feet. And these weren't just any feet — these were first-century, sandal-wearing, callous-covered, manure-stained, twisted, gnarly, untrimmed-toenailed feet. Humble Jesus served the servants by performing a very demeaning chore.

If that sounds too amazing to be true, consider the nature of Jesus Christ.

> Have this attitude in yourselves which was also in Christ Jesus, who, although He existed in the form of God, did not regard equality with God a thing to be grasped, but **emptied Himself**, taking the form of a **bond-servant**, and being made in the likeness of men. Being found in appearance as a man, He **humbled Himself**

by becoming obedient **to the point of death**, even death on a cross (Philippians 2:5–8).

The One who had the right to demand to be served, served others while on earth and He is going to serve you a banquet in heaven. Ponder that the next time you are worried about food.

Clothing

Worried about what to wear? Consider this perspective from paraplegic Joni Eareckson Tada, who cannot clothe herself.

> One thing that I really wish I could do is dress myself. It can be a little frustrating at times. I wish I could do it for myself because it is, after all, a rather private thing, rather personal. And so, in the past, I have always looked at it as a problem, but thankfully, this "problem" has always driven me to God for help. But isn't it just like the Lord Jesus to give not only grace when we need it, but help and insight.
>
> I was reading in Revelation how one day we will be "clothed in righteousness." I was intrigued by that word "clothed." So I did a quick word search and found myself in Galatians chapter 3, verse 27, where it says:
>
> "You who were baptized into Christ have clothed yourselves with Christ" (Galatians 3:27; NIV).
>
> And that got me really going. I looked up more references and I found Isaiah chapter 61 where it says:
>
> "I delight greatly in the Lord; my soul rejoices in my God, for he has clothed me with garments of salvation, and arrayed me in a robe of righteousness" (Isaiah 61:10).
>
> I tell you, all these verses really brightened my spirit and they got me to thinking: why, when the Bible talks about our righteousness, does it always say that God clothes us? Like something he puts on us or does to us. (I mean, even way back in the Garden of Eden, it was God who provided a sacrifice and, therefore, the skins to clothe Adam and Eve after the Fall).
>
> And then it hit me: Garments of salvation and robes of righteousness. This is something we absolutely cannot provide for ourselves.

> God provides the salvation and the righteousness; oh, yes, we can clothe ourselves with Christ as it says in Galatians, but it's His righteousness, not ours. And so, righteousness is something which God does to us and for us. There is nothing in ourselves; we just cannot get ourselves dressed, so to speak, in righteousness. And if we did, it says that our righteousness would be as filthy rags — can you imagine what you'd look like if you had to dress yourself in that? I mean, just picture a garment, a robe made out of your own filthy rags. Yuck!
>
> Suddenly I gained a whole new appreciation for not being able to get myself dressed. Someone else has to do that for me. That very personal and private function is performed by God Himself. Well, you can imagine how blessed I was by that simple, sweet insight.
>
> Praise God, I cannot get myself dressed in robes of righteousness. Hallelujah, I am so happy I cannot dress myself in garments of righteousness. And, friend, you can't get yourself dressed either, someone else has to do that for you. And a Someone with a capital 'S' has graciously and mercifully done that for you. The Lord Jesus Christ is your garment of praise, and when you put on Him, you put on His righteousness. And you know what? You couldn't be decked out in a better pair of clothes.[1]

The next time you fret about fashions, ponder the robe of righteousness you have been given and imagine the heavenly garments you will one day wear.

Money

Is cash your concern? Are you worried about your bank account? Your investments? Then contemplate what your eternal retirement package looks like.

- You will be overlooking a sea of glass (Revelation 15:2).
- You will be walking on streets of gold (Revelation 21:21).
- You will be living in a gated community with an entrance made of jewels (Revelation 21:21).

As marvelous as those amenities are, the greatest treasure in heaven is the One you will spend eternity getting to know. You will have an eternity to

1. http://www.joniandfriends.org/radio/5-minute/clothed-righteousness/.

plumb the depths of the unfathomable riches that are in Jesus Christ (Ephesians 3:8).

We are paupers who have been made rich in ways the world cannot fathom. Forbes annually lists the richest people in the world, but this list pales in comparison to another list of wealthy people catalogued in the Lamb's Book of Life. If your name is in that book, then you share in the riches of Jesus Christ who is the greatest treasure of all.

Work

Is work making you bonkers? Do your customers or coworkers frazzle you? Are you frustrated by the toil of labor? Then dwell on the job you will have in heaven.

God ordained work prior to the Fall (Genesis 2:15). Work is not sinful; work is good. God is a working God and we are made in His image and we have been chosen to do good works.

> For we are His workmanship, created in Christ Jesus **for good works**, which God prepared **beforehand** so that we would walk in them (Ephesians 2:10).

But here's the problem: sin. Because of sin, we toil at labor (Genesis 3:17). Because of sin, stuff breaks, emails get lost, computers freeze up, people fail. This can cause no small amount of anxiety.

A number of years ago, laborers in Great Britain were asked if they would prefer receiving a raise or an enhanced job title. The majority preferred having a better title than cash. Your title in heaven will be: Servant of the Most High God.

When you do your job in heaven (Revelation 22:3), you will enjoy fruitful labor without the toil and frustration that the Curse foisted on work (Genesis 3:17–19). When work makes you anxious, just think about your new, sinless, totally fulfilling and immensely satisfying employment in heaven.

Family and Relationships

There is no pain like family pain. In heaven, you won't have any familial sorrow. There will be no conflict, no disappointed tears, no fighting, no misunderstandings, no disagreements, no gossip, no anger, no hatred, no yelling, no nasty remarks, no wounds.

If you are anxious about spending time with your relatives for the holidays, you won't have that anxiety in heaven where everyone is intimately united in Jesus Christ, living in perfect joy, bliss, and harmony. For the first time ever, you will be in one big, happy family.

Fear of Man

Do you worry about what people on earth think about you? Then remember that you will be reigning with Jesus Christ for all of eternity.

> It is a trustworthy statement: for if we died with Him, we will also **live with Him**; if we endure, we will also **reign with Him** (2 Timothy 2:11–12).

Who cares what the servants think when the King says, "You are mine, I love you and you are going to reign with Me"? Why are you worried about what classmates, neighbors, or coworkers think about you when you know that you are going to reign with Jesus Christ?

Your life is hidden with Christ and you are going to serve Him and reign with Him in glory.

> Therefore if you have been raised up with Christ, **keep seeking the things above**, where Christ is, seated at the right hand of God. **Set your mind on the things above**, not on the things that are on earth. For you have died and your life is **hidden with Christ** in God. When Christ, who is our life, is revealed, then you also will be revealed **with Him in glory** (Colossians 3:1–4).

Are you anxious? Trust God's promises. Think about the place He has prepared for you. Chew on the thought of being served a banquet by the King. Then watch your anxiety over temporal concerns turn into thoughts of heavenly joys.

Our Heaven, Our Glory, and Our Portion!

James Smith

We shall be *forever with Christ!*

Now, we have to mourn His absence. . . . But He has provided something better for us — even to dwell forever in His presence — which will constitute our Heaven, our glory, and our portion!

O with what rapture shall we fix and feast our eyes upon Him, and how will the thought that we are to be *forever* with Him — thrill through our souls, and open ten thousand gushing streams of unutterable delight and joy! O with what joy shall we hear Him say, "*Come*, you who are blessed of My Father!"

The presence of Jesus will
dissipate all gloom,
disperse all slavish fears,
chase away all darkness,
free from all pain,
deliver from all sorrow,
preserve from all sickness,
raise us above all temptations, and
fill us with unspeakably glorious joy.

Here on earth, we may be cast down — for the way is rough and our trials are many. Here we may mourn the absence of our God — but the love of Jesus will soon rescue us, and we shall be received into His presence to abide forever!

To be *with* Christ — to be with Christ *forever* — this comprises all that we now desire, and all that we can wish![2]

2. http://www.gracegems.org/2011/09/our.html.

Chapter 7

Anxiety Reliever #3: You Know God

There are only two types of people in the world: the people who know God and the people who don't. If you don't know God, you should be anxious, but if you know Him, you have absolutely nothing to worry about.

Knowing God is Jesus' anxiety reliever number three.

> If you had really known me, you would know who my Father is. From now on, **you know Him** and Have **seen Him** (John 14:7; NLT)!

Of all the people to know in the world, you know God.

- You may not know Bill Gates, but you know God.
- You may not know Brad and Angelina, but you know God.
- You may not know the president of the United States, but you know God.

You may not have any famous people on your speed-dial, but you know God.

In Adam

When we are conceived, we inherit a nature that was purchased for us by our federal head, Adam. We are conceived in sin, born in sin, live in sin, and we will die in sin and receive the due reward for our sinning.

The unregenerate, unsaved man is in Adam. This man lives to serve his master, Satan. This man's best friend is his sin. This man's destiny is hell. This man's enemy is God Himself. In 1671, Joseph Alleine painted this man's eternal picture.

> I myself, the Sovereign Lord, am now **your enemy!** (Ezekiel 5:8).
> Unconverted sinner!
>
> You are not only without God — but God is against you! . . . As there is no friend like Him — so there is no enemy like Him. As much as heaven is above the earth, omnipotence above impotence, so much more terrible is it to fall into the hands of the living God, than into the paws of bears and lions, yes, furies or devils! God Himself will be your tormentor! . . .
>
> Who or what shall deliver you out of His hands? . . .
>
> God Himself is your enemy! Oh where will you go? Where will you shelter yourself?
>
> The infinite God is engaged against you! . . .
>
> He hates all workers of iniquity.
>
> "As surely as I live, when I sharpen My flashing sword and begin to carry out justice, I will bring vengeance on My enemies and repay those who hate Me" (Deuteronomy 32:40-41)!
>
> The power of God is mounted like a mighty cannon against you.
>
> Sinner. . . . There is no escaping His hands — no breaking loose from His prison.
>
> O consider this, you that forget God, lest He tear you in pieces, and there be none to deliver (Psalm 50:22)![1]

That is the fate of every man and woman who is born and remains in Adam; God is not their friend, He is their enemy.

In Christ

If you have repented and placed your faith in Jesus, then God has plucked you out of Adam and placed you into Jesus Christ. That means you are not God's enemy, but have been made His friend.

- If you are in Christ, you are no longer a hell-bound sinner but a glory-bound saint.
- If you are in Christ, you are no longer an alien from God, but you have been brought near.

1. Excerpts from http://gracegems.org/28/alarm_to_the_unconverted6.htm.

- If you are in Christ, you are no longer a servant of Satan, but you are a bondservant of the King.
- If you are in Christ, you do not walk in darkness, but you are a child of the light.

Because you are in Christ, there is one answer to all of these questions:

- Are you famous?
- Who do you know?
- How many people know you?
- How many Twitter followers do you have?

For the person who is in Christ, the answer to all of those questions is: WHO CARES?

- Who cares what people know you; you know God.
- Who cares how many people know you; you know God.
- Who cares how many likes you get on Facebook; you know God.

You don't just know about God, you know Him personally. You don't just know what God is like, you actually know Him. If that isn't knocking your socks off, then we need to take a moment to fix your gaze on the invisible God. How can we look at a God who is invisible? By seeing that He has made Himself known to us physically.

Because of Jesus Christ, you don't have to imagine a spirit in the sky. Jesus Christ put on human flesh and dwelt among us so we could know exactly what God is like.

> He [Jesus] is the **image of the invisible God**, the firstborn of all creation. . . . For it was the Father's good pleasure for **all the fullness to dwell in Him**, and through Him to reconcile all things to Himself, having made peace through the blood of His cross; through Him, I say, whether things on earth or things in heaven (Colossians 1:15–20).

Do you want to know what God is like? Look at Jesus. You can't get a better understanding of God than by studying Jesus. So what do we see in Jesus? We see a loving, humble, caring, giving, sacrificing God who gets you.

Jesus is sympathetic (Hebrews 2:17): You are not going through anything Jesus has not endured . . . He even endured far worse. Every struggle you have,

He had. Every heartache you face, He endured far more. Every disappointment you experience, Jesus felt far worse. You will never face anything harder, scarier, more challenging, or more difficult than Jesus. He gets you.

Jesus is forgiving (Luke 23:34): Are you anxious because you have committed a sin that you never want anyone to discover? Jesus knows about it and stands with overflowing mercy and willingness to forgive you and save you to the uttermost (Hebrews 7:25).

Jesus is loving (John 15:13): Not only is Jesus willing to forgive your dirtiest of dirty sins, but He loves you so much He actually gives you credit for His righteousness. You are no longer the dirtiest kid on the block, you are now the citizen of the century.

Jesus is compassionate (Luke 7:13): When Jesus saw people who were hurting, He looked at them with compassion — not disdain, not annoyance, not frustration. Jesus had compassion on them and He has compassion on us.

Jesus is gentle (Luke 18:16): Jesus put little children on His lap and they sat still. They didn't run away. They didn't scream for their mothers. Why? Because Jesus was gentle with children, and He is gentle with us.

Jesus is caring (Luke 6:19): Jesus virtually wiped out disease while He ministered for three years because He cared for people. And He cares for you.

Is it any wonder that crowds flocked to be with Jesus? God in the flesh was the most amazing person they had ever experienced. Jesus was not capricious, mean, vindictive, cruel, short-tempered or cold. Every attribute that God possesses, Jesus personified. And you know Him.

Jesus perfectly personified the fruit of the Spirit in every possible way (Galatians 5:22-23).

- Jesus loved perfectly.
- Jesus was totally joyful.
- Jesus had an amazing peace about Him.
- Jesus was perfectly patient.
- Jesus was profoundly kind and good.
- Jesus was more faithful than a brother.
- Jesus was gentler than a mother.
- Jesus was always firmly under control and never managed by circumstances or events.

That is the One God wants to conform you to. Can you imagine how it would feel to be more like Jesus? If you would like to be more like Him, then study Jesus in the Word and you will become like Him.

> But we all, with unveiled face, beholding as in a mirror the glory of the Lord, are **being transformed into the same image** from glory to glory, just as from the Lord, the Spirit (2 Corinthians 3:18).

Jesus is the most amazing man to ever live because He was God-in-flesh. When we study the man Jesus Christ, we get to see what God is like because Jesus possessed and still possesses all the attributes of God:

God is patient, and so is Jesus (2 Peter 3:9): Jesus doesn't get exasperated with you. Ever. He is unwaveringly patient with you as you stumble, fumble, and fall.

God is immutable, and so is Jesus (Malachi 3:6): When Jesus promised that He would never leave you nor forsake you (Matthew 28:20; Hebrews 13:5), He will not; He cannot change His mind about you.

God is all wise, and so is Jesus (Romans 11:33): Does Jesus know how to handle your situation? Of course He does, He is all wise.

God is faithful, and so is Jesus (1 Corinthians 1:9): When Jesus said that He is going to prepare a place for you (John 14:2), He is going to make sure you get there (1 Corinthians 1:8; Philippians 1:6).

God is self-existent, and so is Jesus (Exodus 3:14): Jesus doesn't need anyone or anything to make His life better. The fact that He doesn't need us is great news. Why? Because God loves us even though we have nothing to offer Him. That means His love for you is not contingent on your performance, His love is based on His character of love (1 John 4:8).

God is omnipotent, and so is Jesus (Psalm 147:5): You never need to worry about Jesus' ability to help you get through your trial. He is omnipotent.

God is just, and so is Jesus (2 Thessalonians 1:6): If someone is sinning against you, you do not need to retaliate or get even or worry that he/she will get away with it (Romans 12:19). The God of justice will avenge the sins committed against you.

That is your God. That is the God you get to know if you are in Christ.

It gets even better. Not only do you know God, but He knows you. He knows you by name. He knows every single thing about you and He chooses to love you.

Perspective

Think of it like this:

- You don't know any Academy Award winners, but you know the most famous person in history, Jesus Christ.
- You don't know any millionaires, but you know the One who owns the cattle on a thousand hills.
- You don't know the finest surgeons in the world, but you know the Great Physician who can heal you with a simple word.
- You don't know anyone at the Pentagon, but you know the One who can melt every army on the planet with a thought.
- You don't know any mobsters who can pay a special visit to the person who is troubling you, but you do know the righteous, omnipotent God who is going to judge every thug, every sinner, and every person who has ever sinned against you.

The next time calamity strikes, remember that you know God.

The next time the check bounces, remember that you know God.

The next time you fear for your life, remember that you know God.

The next time your prodigal runs away, remember that you know God.

The next time your spouse disappoints you, remember that you know God.

When you are anxious, "Turn your eyes upon Jesus, look long upon His wonderful face, and the things of this world will grow strangely dim, in the light of His glory and grace."[2]

When hard things happen to you, you can spend your nights walking the floor, or you can study the God you know and let the knowledge of His love, power, and wisdom remove your anxiety.

You don't have to worry about anything or anyone ever again. You know God, He knows you, and He is for you. You are in good hands.

2. Helen H. Lemmel, "Turn Your Eyes upon Jesus."

God, the Portion of His People

James Smith

Tried Christian, you are not an orphan! You have a Father! God, in all the glory of his nature and perfections, is your Father! He has adopted you for his own. He has regenerated you by his Spirit. He has called you out of the world, and has promised to do a father's part unto you. He says, "I will be a Father unto you."

Do you need advice? Consult your Father.

Do you need supplies? Ask them of your Father.

Are you tormented with cares? Cast them on your Father.

Are you alarmed at foes? Cry unto your Father.

Do your difficulties appear insurmountable? Appeal to your Father.

God is not merely a Father in name; he has a Father's nature. He not only calls us his sons and daughters, but wishes us to act towards him as such. We should exercise confidence in his love; we should trust in his word; we should appeal to his paternal heart; we should look for our supplies from his hand.

Believer, whatever trials may befall you, whatever troubles may come upon you, whatever enemies may rise up against you, whatever changes may take place in your circumstances, one thing can never befall you—you can never be fatherless; therefore you can never be friendless. You are God's child, however poor your circumstances, or trying your path. What an unspeakable mercy![3]

3. http://www.gracegems.org/C/Our_Father.htm.

Chapter 8

Anxiety Reliever #4: You Can Hear from God

In the 19th century it was a thrill to receive a telegraph that contained even the briefest message. In the 20th century we jumped when our telephones rang; and three words made our hearts go pitter-patter: "You've got mail."

Today, we wake up and immediately check our cell phones for texts and emails. We love hearing from people, especially important people. That is why these words from Jesus should make us downright giddy.

> The **words** that I say to you I do not speak on My own initiative (John 14:10).

When you read the inspired word of God, you are actually receiving a message directly from God to you. If getting texts makes you happy, reading your Bible should thrill your soul.

When you crack open your Bible, you are reading the very words of God. It doesn't matter if the ink is red or black, you are reading the inspired, infallible, inerrant, sufficient word of God. Whoa.

> **All** Scripture is **inspired by God** and profitable for teaching, for reproof, for correction, for training in righteousness; so that the man of God may be adequate, equipped for every good work (2 Timothy 3:16–17).

If that verse is true, and it is, then you have everything you need in the Bible to help you control your emotions. That's what Psalm 119 says too.

Psalm 119

The longest chapter in the Bible touts the Scriptures as being a soothing balm for the Psalmist's troubled emotions. He doesn't reveal what is rocking his boat, but the author of Psalm 119 is clearly under pressure.

Repeatedly, the Psalmist says that his soul is "crushed with longing" (vs. 20), and that he is being treated poorly by somebody (vs. 22). So how does the Psalmist find comfort? You guessed it — from the Word of God.

> My soul weeps because of grief; strengthen me according to **Your word** (Psalm 119:28).

That theme is repeated for 176 verses. Whatever is getting the Psalmist's goat, he makes it clear that there is only one solution for his situation; the Word of God.

> My soul cleaves to the **dust**;
> Revive me according to **Your word**.
> I have told of my ways, and You have answered me;
> Teach me **Your statutes**.
> Make me understand the way of **Your precepts**,
> So I will meditate on **Your wonders**.
> My soul weeps because of **grief**;
> Strengthen me according to **Your word** (Psalm 119:25–28).

Notice what the Psalmist does *not* prescribe for comfort. He does not recommend chitchat, reading inspirational stories, drinking alcohol, or getting a mani-pedi. The Psalmist recommends one cure and one cure alone: the Word of God.

- What do you need when your heart is feeling blue? You need to hear from God through His Word.
- What do you need when you are worried about tomorrow? You need to read His Word today.
- What do you need if you fear man? You need a word from God.

The formula is clear: if you want peace, you must read the Bible to acquire knowledge. Hearing from God through His Word is crucial if we are going to have our brains informed by truth.

In order to be persuaded that God wants to do exceedingly more than stabilize your wobbly emotions, consider these verses.

Verse One: 2 Corinthians 3:18

When Moses descended the mountain with a glowing face due to seeing the glory of God, he put a veil over his face. The Jews who met Moses could only see a fading glory behind a veil. You and I get to see the glory of God revealed in Jesus Christ without a veil.

> But we all, with unveiled face, **beholding** as in a mirror the glory of the Lord, are being transformed into the same image from **glory to glory**, just as from the Lord, the Spirit (2 Corinthians 3:18).

When you and I stare into the face of Jesus by studying His words, we are actually changed "from glory to glory." We progressively become like the object we are studying.

Verse Two: Colossians 3:9–10

We are born in sin. When we are born again, God changes our hearts and desires. More than that, He actually changes us into His image.

> . . . since you laid aside the old self with its evil practices, and have put on the new self who is being renewed to a **true knowledge** according to the image of the One who created him (Colossians 3:9–10).

How does God change us to be like Him? By giving us true knowledge. Where is true knowledge found? The Bible.

Verse Three: 2 Peter 1:2–4

God has given us all the power we need to become like Jesus.

> Grace and **peace** be multiplied to you in the **knowledge of God and of Jesus** our Lord; seeing that His divine **power** has granted to us everything pertaining to life and godliness, through the **true knowledge of Him** who called us by His own glory and excellence. For by these He has granted to us His precious and magnificent **promises**, so that by them you **may become partakers of the divine**

> **nature**, having escaped the corruption that is in the world by lust (2 Peter 1:2–4).

Those three verses explode with great news for us.

- We get peace (wholeness, peace of mind) through increased knowledge of God and Jesus (vs. 2).
- We have all the power we need to be godly; we don't need to ask for more (vs. 3).
- When we consider His most precious promise, Jesus, we become partakers of the divine nature. We don't become gods, but we do become like God (vs. 4).

How amazing is God? He wants you to look like the magnificent image bearer that He made you to be. He wants you to look like Himself.

VERSE FOUR: ROMANS 12:2

God wants to transform our minds so that we no longer act and think like the fallen sinners we are.

> And do not be conformed to this world, but **be transformed** by the **renewing of your mind**, so that you may prove what the will of God is, that which is good and acceptable and perfect (Romans 12:2).

These four verses tell us what God wants to do with us. He doesn't want to simply eliminate your anxious thoughts: He wants to remake you. Fix you. Change you. Improve you. Conform you into His very image.

God does not just zap you and change you; God's Holy Spirit changes you as you read His Holy Spirit–inspired Word. Want change? Read your Bible. And read it right!

Unfortunately, many people read the Bible wrong and never find the comfort they seek.

SIX ENCOURAGEMENTS

Charles Hodge once wrote, "The Bible is so simple that small children can understand it, and it is so profound that studies by the wisest theologians will never exhaust its riches."[1] The Bible is no ordinary book; it is at once

1. https://mybible.com/covers/343.

simple and yet it can be confusing. Few things will trip up a committed Bible reader quite like getting confused or interpreting the Bible wrongly. Here are some ditches we want to avoid as we read the greatest seller of all time.

Only Apply the Promises That Are for Us

There is a song that claims, "Every promise in the book is mine, every chapter, every verse, every line." Um, no, not exactly.

For starters, many promises of the Bible are threats aimed at unbelievers. Many of the promises of the Bible are curses. Many of the promises of the Bible promise harm and not good. You don't want those promises. For instance, you don't want this promise:

> Behold, I am sending upon them the sword, famine and pestilence (Jeremiah 29:17).

When reading the Bible, study the context to make sure that the promise that is given is actually intended for us. Just as you don't want the promise in Jeremiah 29:17, you can't take good promises that were not written for you.

> "For I know the plans that I have for you," declares the Lord, "plans for welfare and not for calamity to give you **a future and a hope**" (Jeremiah 29:11).

While that promise sure sounds good, it wasn't actually given to us. Context tells us this promise was made to the Jews in exile whom God promised to return to the Promised Land because of God's faithfulness to His Abrahamic covenant.

Besides, the rest of the Bible makes clear that believers will experience trials, tribulations, and temptations (John 16:33). Job learned that lesson, and we should too. Good interpretive skills are needed to make sure we don't rely on promises that were not given to us.

Read the Promises for You with Faith

When we read promises that are intended for New Testament saints, we too easily think they are for other Christians, but certainly not us. When God promises that He "will never leave you or forsake you," He means it. Trust Him. Believe that God means what He says and He never reneges (James 1:17).

Focus Primarily on God

To be certain, we can learn much about ourselves when we read the Bible. We should happily consume that knowledge (whether good or bad), but if we only search the Scriptures looking for stories and promises for us, then we miss the source of our strength. Focusing on who God is and what He has done is the knowledge that we need to trust the promises He has made for us.

If I told you that I was going to give you a thousand dollars, you would feel pretty good. But as time went by and no money showed up, you would begin to doubt. You could make yourself feel better by repeating, "I'm gonna get a thousand bucks," but after a while, you are going to lose hope. However, if you regularly read your local newspaper about all of the people I gave a thousand dollars to, your hope would be revived as you read about my character.

When you are anxious, yes, read about God's promises to comfort you; but also read about God's character and ability to do what He says He promises to do.

- When you are worried about the future, read the hundreds of prophecies that God fulfilled.
- When you are frightened of your enemies, read how God destroyed every army that ever opposed Him.
- When you doubt that God is able to rescue you from your situation, read how God was able to deliver the Jews from Egypt by sending ten plagues.
- When you fear there is no way of escape, read the harrowing stories of David's near misses with mad King Saul.

Studying God's omnipotence and benevolence will help you know that God is able and your hope is rightly placed.

Remember How the Bible Works

The Bible is many things, but one thing it is not is a magic book. The Bible doesn't miraculously make everything better simply by reading it. The Bible is meant to be studied, believed, and applied. As we do that, the Holy Spirit progressively changes us into the image of the Son. Do not be discouraged if your anxiety doesn't immediately disappear.

Read It as More than a History Book or Morality Tale

The Bible is a fascinating tour of history in the land of Israel, but the Bible is far more than a history book. The Bible recalls the history of the nation of Israel so we can believe in the Jewish Messiah. Be careful that you don't get carried away in cool stories like Noah's ark, David and Bathsheba, and the betrayal of Judas without remembering that the Bible is more than history — it is the story of God's plan of redemption.

While there are many moral lessons in the Bible, watch out for the trap of moralism. God still commands Christians to obey, but if we forget the motivation for our good behavior, then we will quickly become Pharisees and not Christians.

Oh, and don't forget, there are no allegories in the Bible. When Jesus said He would be in the belly of the earth just like Jonah was in the belly of a big fish, He meant that there was an actual Jonah and an actual big fish. The Bible records history, not fairy tales.

Remember that God Is as Good as He Says He Is

It is stunningly easy to read that God loves us without actually absorbing that fact. This happens for multiple reasons.

- We see and hear silly preachers abuse promises of God's love for us, so we tend to shy away from verses like John 3:16.
- We have seen the abuses of churches that only focus on God's love and we shy away from the verses that we think might make us liberal.
- We are not good at being loved.

Whatever the reason, if we don't read the Bible and see God's love for sinners, we miss one of the greatest truths in the Bible.

To be clear, the Bible is about one thing and one thing only: the redemptive work of Jesus Christ. From Genesis 1 to Revelation 22, the Bible relentlessly points to the Cross. God sent His Son to die for sinners to demonstrate His mercy, grace, and loving-kindness. Everything in this universe exists to serve Him and bring Him glory.

However, if we overlook God's love for us as we read the Bible, we miss the very thing He is trying to demonstrate. We also miss a lot of comfort, security, hope, and joy.

It is easy to fall into one of two ditches when we read about God's love. We can focus only on how much He loves us and conclude the universe exists for us. Unfortunately, we can fall into the other ditch of forgetting that God really does love us and we can become rather despondent. In order to appreciate God's true love for us and remain humble, we must read our Bibles with balance.

Read with Balance

When you read that God created the world, read that He created the world for His glory. But don't forget that He also made it for you to enjoy. God created the world for His glory and our benefit.

When you read that God delivered the Jews from Egypt, know that He did that to fulfill His Abrahamic covenant of a land, nation, and Messiah. But remember that He sent a Messiah so you could be forgiven and live. God literally parted a Red Sea for His glory and so you could be saved.

When you read that God provided manna in the wilderness for the Jews to survive, He did that so His Messiah would come out of a holy people. But He also performed that miracle so you could have your sins forgiven by that Messiah.

Don't fall into a ditch thinking that God exists to serve you, but don't fall into the other ditch that says that God does not genuinely care about you. God does everything for His glory, but don't forget that God loves you so much that He also organizes every single event in the universe so you can know Him and be saved by Him.

Psalms

Imagine a planet with no Bible. Imagine living life without ever hearing from God. Imagine living for eight decades never knowing anything about our Maker. Imagine living in perpetual fear because our consciences inform us that our Creator is thoroughly displeased with our behavior.

Now imagine a man or woman on that planet praying,

> Dear Lord, would you please have the third member of the Trinity inspire 40 men during the span of 1,500 years to write a book that has everything we need for life and godliness? Make sure you don't override their personalities and ensure there are no errors

whatsoever. Please give us a completely accurate book that has everything we need for life and godliness. Make sure that nothing is lacking for all people, for all time, to know You and how we might be saved from the wrath that is to come.

And please include 150 chapters of poetry dedicated to helping us have correct emotions. Write them tenderly and in a comforting manner so we can read those chapters when we are inclined to not trust You.

We would consider that a blasphemous prayer. And yet, that is precisely what God has done for us. The Holy Spirit inspired an entire Bible that contains the words of life and words of comfort for you. He even gave us an entire book dedicated to guide our worship and modulate our emotions, the Book of Psalms. What a kind God.

The Book of Psalms is the perfect place to go when you are looking to make sure your feelings are right. No, the Bible doesn't talk about depression (mostly because the word was not used until the 15th century), but the Book of Psalms is loaded with chapters that deal expressly with worry.

The next time you are worried about your enemies, read about God's stunning victories over the enemies of Israel. That is the same God who says, "I am for you." God defeated Israel's treacherous enemies; He can handle your foes too.

> He **smote** many nations
> And **slew** mighty kings,
> Sihon, king of the Amorites,
> And Og, king of Bashan,
> And all the kingdoms of Canaan;
> And He gave their land as a heritage,
> A heritage to Israel His people (Psalm 135:10–12).

The next time you are worried about food and shelter, read this:

> He who dwells in the shelter of the Most High
> Will abide in the shadow of the Almighty.
> I will say to the LORD, "My refuge and my fortress,
> My God, in whom I trust!"
> For it is **He who delivers you** from the snare of the trapper

And from the deadly pestilence.
He will cover you with His pinions,
And under His wings you may seek refuge;
His faithfulness is a **shield and bulwark** (Psalm 91:1–4).

The next time you are worried about the future, read this:

> I will lift up my eyes to the mountains;
> From where shall my help come?
> My help comes from the LORD,
> Who made heaven and earth.
> He **will not allow** your foot to slip;
> He who keeps you will not slumber (Psalm 121:1–3).

The next time you are worried about your children, read this:

> But the loving-kindness of the LORD is from everlasting to everlasting on those who fear Him, and His righteousness to **children's children** (Psalm 103:17).

When your emotions need to be calmed, soothed, energized, or excited, open up the book that the God of all comfort wrote to comfort you, the Psalms.

JESUS

Jesus never sighed, "I am exhausted from walking the floors last night. I am so stressed." Jesus was fully in control of His emotions and He has the ability to help you get your emotions under His control too.

The supreme source of peace is found when you read about the Prince of Peace.

- If you want to be comforted when the waters of life seem to be overtaking you, then watch Jesus lift Peter out of the water when he began to doubt and sink (Matthew 14:28–33).
- If you want to know if your God cares about your children, watch Jesus tenderly bless babies who were brought to Him (Luke 18:15–16).
- If you want to know if God can heal you, watch Jesus heal everyone who came to Him (Matthew 9:35–36).

- If you want to know if God can provide for you, watch Jesus feed thousands of men, women, and children (Matthew 14:13–21).
- If you want to know if your sins can be forgiven, watch Jesus take the beatings and hang on the Cross you deserve (Matthew 27:33–55).

The next time you fret about the future, look into the past and study Jesus; the One who stilled the waters can still your soul. And as you do this, something supernatural is going to happen to you. When you study your Savior, you will not only be comforted, but you will actually be changed. The more you read about Jesus, the more you will become like Him. While God desires to soothe your jangled nerves as you read about His Son, He is far more interested in changing you to have the emotions of His beloved Son.

Three Warnings

The formula is simple: read God's Word, believe it and apply it, and you will be changed. While it seems like it should be easy to be changed by God's Word, we have a tendency to flub it up.

For starters, we have a tendency to think that knowing facts about God is the same as knowing Him. It is not.

If you know that your mother is making your favorite dinner, but you never go home to sit at the table, you have knowledge but you are not enjoying what has been done for you. If you know that the Holy Spirit wants to comfort you through His Word but you don't trust Him, you won't be comforted.

Second, knowing theology and believing theology is not the same thing. Knowing creeds and systematic theology is good, but if it is not the truth that you are building your life on, then you will never be strengthened by the knowledge you possess.

Third, knowing theology and being warmed and changed by theology are two different things. When you read your Bible, you are not reading a story or fable. God actually spoke the world into existence and He actually destroyed it with a global Flood. God actually sent ten plagues. God actually sent His Son to die for you.

As we read His Word, we have to be taking our own theological temperature.

- If our study of God is not producing a change in thinking, acting, and feeling, then we are not studying right.

- If our study of God is not leading us to increasing trust, then we are merely storing knowledge.
- If our study of God isn't leading us to worship, then we are merely amassing data.
- If our study of God isn't causing us to trust Him more and fear man less, then we are merely becoming theologians.

But if you read God's Word, believe it, and apply it, your thinking will be changed and your heart will soar.

God's Word is like an oxygen mask that falls before you when your plane hits turbulence. When you have the sufficient, inerrant, infallible, inspired Word of God, you have everything you need for life and godliness. Drink it in and it will quench your thirst.

Search the Scriptures!

George Everard, 1878

The word *Bible* signifies *Book*; and when we call it the Bible, we mean that it is *the Book of books* — the *best* Book, the *wisest* Book, the Book that will do us the most good of any in the world!

If all the other books in the world were destroyed, however great and irreparable the loss — if men still had the Bible, they would be far better off than if this were destroyed and all other books remained.

It is the Book that alone can tell:
how sin can be forgiven,
how temptation can be overcome,
how trouble and sorrow can be met,
how tears can be wiped away, and
how death can be the gate of everlasting life.
It is indeed the best companion . . .
for days of trial,
for the day of sickness, and
for the hour when we must part from all below!
Oh what a treasure is a well-read Bible! It is . . .
a mine of gold, a hive full of honey,
a field covered with a rich harvest.
It is a tree of life, of which every twig bears precious fruit.
It is an ocean full of pearls.
It is a river full of the purest water of life.
It is a sun whose beams warm and cheer the heart.

It is a bright star that can guide the pilgrim through the darkest night.

It is a granary stored with the finest of the wheat.

It is a medicine-chest, from which we may find a remedy for every malady of the soul.

All this and much more, is the Bible to those who love to search it and explore the depths of heavenly wisdom which it contains.

Dear reader, whatever you forget, never, never forget to read something out of this precious Book day by day.[2]

2. http://www.gracegems.org/2015/12/scriptures.html.

Chapter 9

Anxiety Reliever #5: You Have a Comforter

What in the world could possibly be better than living on earth with Jesus Christ? Answer: anxiety reliever number 5.

> And I will pray the Father, and he shall give you another **Comforter**, that he may abide with you **for ever** (John 14:16; KJV).

The Father created us. Jesus redeemed us. The Holy Spirit saves us. But the Holy Spirit does even more than that. Once He saves us, He dwells in us, reveals the truth of God's Word to us, sanctifies us, and comforts us. That is why Jesus called the Holy Spirit the Comforter. The word that Jesus used to describe Him is *paraclete* — one called alongside to help and be an advocate.

That means you have the Holy Spirit of God dwelling in you (1 Corinthians 3:16; 2 Timothy 1:14), and one of His "jobs" is to comfort you when you start to feel anxious. Understanding how He does this is crucial if we are going to be comforted.

> But the Helper [this is the same Greek word, *paraclete*], the Holy Spirit, whom the Father will send in My name, He **will teach you all things**, and bring to your remembrance all that I said to you. Peace I leave with you; My peace I give to you; not as the world gives do I give to you. **Do not let your heart be troubled**, nor let it be fearful (John 14:26–27).

The Holy Spirit comforts you when He teaches you all things. What are "all things" that He wants to teach you? All of the things written in the Word (2 Timothy 3:16–17; Psalm 119:65–68). This makes perfect sense because the Holy Spirit Himself inspired the Word (2 Peter 1:21).

Consider all of the roles of the Holy Spirit and how He completes those tasks.

1. The Holy Spirit saves through the proclamation of His Word (Romans 10:17).
2. The Holy Spirit teaches us His Word (1 Corinthians 2:13–14).
3. The Holy Spirit sanctifies us through His Word (1 Peter 1:3; 2 Thessalonians 2:13).

Our God is not mystical. God doesn't sprinkle fairy dust on us to calm us down when we are anxious. God is a cognitive God who works in us through our brains. His ordained means to accomplish that is the Holy Spirit–inspired Word.

What Could Be Better?

If you could go back in time and meet anyone in history, you would undoubtedly say, "Jesus." And if you went back in time and were able to spend three years with "God in Flesh," He would tell you that there is something better than being with Him.

Most certainly you would think, "What could be better than being with Jesus?" His answer is: the Holy Spirit.

In His physical body, Jesus could only be with a limited number of people at a time. The bigger the crowd, the less personal attention you received from the man, Jesus Christ. The Holy Spirit, however, dwells personally in the heart of every believer. That is why Jesus said this to the disciples:

> "But now I am going to Him who sent Me; and none of you asks Me, 'Where are You going?' But because I have said these things to you, **sorrow has filled your heart**. But I tell you the truth, it is to **your advantage** that I go away; for if I do not go away, the **Helper** will not come to you; but if I go, I will **send Him** to you. And He, when He comes, will convict the world concerning sin and righteousness and judgment; concerning sin, because they do

> not believe in Me; and concerning righteousness, because I go to the Father and you **no longer see Me**; and concerning judgment, because the ruler of this world has been judged.
>
> "I have many more things to say to you, but you **cannot bear them now**. But when He, the **Spirit of truth**, comes, He will **guide you into all the truth**; for He will not speak on His own initiative, but whatever He hears, He will speak; and **He will disclose to you what is to come**. He will glorify Me, for He will take of Mine and will **disclose it to you**. All things that the Father has are Mine; therefore I said that He takes of Mine and will **disclose** it to you" (John 16:5–15).

Notice how Jesus tells us the Holy Spirit comforts us: through His Word. When you are feeling anxious and you ask God, "Please let me know what I am supposed to do," His response is, "Read your Bible!"

- Aroma therapy might make you relax while you smell the oils, but the Holy Spirit–inspired Word changes your thinking and sets your heart on the right path.
- A Jacuzzi might temporarily relieve stress, but the Holy Spirit will progressively teach you to trust Him when the world is crashing in.
- Changing your emotions by running away might work for a season, but the Holy Spirit will actually transform your ability to deal with the circumstances that cause your emotions to be in flux.

Did you notice Jesus' compassion when He promised the disciples something better was coming? He observed that "sorrow had filled their hearts," and He lovingly determined to not share more information with them that would further grieve them. Your Savior is kind. He is not mean.

- Jesus never yelled at the disciples. He will never yell at you.
- Jesus never mocked the disciples for being thick. He will not mock you.
- Jesus never harangued the disciples for their lack of obedience. He will not scold you either.

Have you ever read anything about Jesus that would cause you to think, "He's going to make fun of me"? Your God is for you, He loves you and He wants to help you.

Your Savior knows that you and I are weak. Your Savior knows that you and I are frail. Your Savior will respond to you the way that He responded to the disciples — lovingly.

Perhaps you think that Jesus is nice even though you are weak, but the Father is kind of crabby. Perhaps you have that opinion of your Heavenly Father because of the failures of your earthly father. Then you need to have your mind changed about Him.

THE TRINITY

First of all, God is three persons, yet One God. He does not suffer from multiple personality disorder or bi-polar disease. Each person of the Godhead enjoys the same attributes in equal measure. We make a mistake when we think the Father can be mean but Jesus is nice. Both are equally just and equally compassionate. Remember, Jesus is the visible image of the invisible God (Colossians 1:15). When you see Jesus being tender with the disciples, that means the Father will be tender with you too.

If you are in Christ, never, ever fear running to your Father. The parable of the prodigal son promises that He will be running toward you (Luke 15:11–32).

POWER

You have more power in you than you are aware of. Sinful anxiety does not have to be your master (Romans 6:14). The Holy Spirit is in you, aiding you, strengthening you, and changing you (Galatians 5:22–23).

You may have a tendency to think that Jesus kept every law, did every miracle, and always acted without sin simply because He is God. That is not accurate. The God-man Jesus was obedient not by His own power, but by the power of the Holy Spirit. Jesus performed miracles by the power of the Holy Spirit. Jesus' emotions were always appropriate because the Holy Spirit of God empowered Him.

- Jesus was conceived by the power of the Holy Spirit (Matthew 1:18).
- Jesus was anointed by the Holy Spirit at His baptism (Luke 3:21–22).
- Jesus began His ministry "full of the Holy Spirit" (Luke 4:1).
- Jesus had the Holy Spirit "without measure" (John 3:34).

- Jesus cast out demons by the power of the Holy Spirit (Matthew 12:28).
- Jesus was raised from the dead by the power of the Holy Spirit (Romans 8:11).

That is profoundly great news for Christians because we have the same Holy Spirit empowering us who empowered Jesus to be perfectly obedient. You have no less power available to you than Jesus did (Romans 8:11–17; Galatians 5:16–24).

To be clear, we still sin, but we don't have to sin. You don't have to worry. You don't have to fear the future. You don't have to be controlled by your emotions; the Holy Spirit can control you. Of course, this raises an important question: can we get more of the Holy Spirit?

> May the God of hope fill you with **all joy and peace in believing**, so that you may abound in hope by the power of the Holy Spirit (Romans 15:13).

We get more of the Holy Spirit by believing more in God. How do we believe more in God? By reading and obeying the Word the Holy Spirit inspired.

Alcohol vs. the Holy Spirit

How many people try to comfort themselves through drugs or alcohol? The Bible offers us a much better remedy: being filled with the Holy Spirit.

> And **do not get drunk** with wine, for that is dissipation, but **be filled with the Spirit** (Ephesians 5:18).

Rather than finding comfort by numbing our senses, God wants our emotions to be under the control of the Holy Spirit by being filled with the Holy Spirit.

How does being filled with the Holy Spirit keep our emotions from turning blue? Because He is the Spirit of JOY! Galatians 5:22–23 lists the fruit of the Spirit and one of those fruits is joy.

> The kingdom of God is not eating and drinking, but righteousness and peace and **joy in the Holy Spirit** (Romans 14:17).

Joy is exactly what the disciples were filled with when they were filled with the Spirit.

> The disciples were continually filled with **joy** and with the **Holy Spirit** (Acts 13:52).

If you want more joy, you need more Holy Spirit. To get more of the Holy Spirit, you need more of His Word. When you read His Word, the Holy Spirit will control you more and more and you will have more and more joy.

There is really only one reason you and I have sinful anxiety — because we do not avail ourselves of everything our gracious God has provided for us to have victory over sin. If your sinful anxiety won't go away, it is only because you are not being obedient and partaking of God's provisions for overcoming your anxiety.

- If your anxiety is persistent, it is because you are not persistently studying His Word.
- If you are overrun by worry, it is because you are filled with yourself and not being filled by the Holy Spirit of joy.
- If you continue to sin by worrying, you have no one to blame but yourself. God has provided all of the tools you need to overcome your anxiety.

You could start mortifying your sinful anxiety today, right now. You cannot do this on your own because you do not have the strength. But the Holy Spirit of God does. Avail yourself of His power by studying His Word, trusting His Word, and obeying His Word.

You Have an Advocate

Knowing that you have an advocate should bring you great joy. You have someone who is presently pleading your case in heaven. As you read this, the Holy Spirit is actually interceding for you.

> In the same way the Spirit also **helps our weakness**; for we do not know how to pray as we should, but the **Spirit Himself intercedes** for us with groanings too deep for words; and He who searches the hearts knows what the mind of the Spirit is, because **He intercedes for the saints according to the will of God** (Romans 8:27–27).

To paraphrase Robert Murray McCheyne, if you could hear the Holy Spirit praying for you in the next room, you would not fear a million enemies.[1]

1. http://www.mcheyne.info/quotes.php.

- What do you fear? The Holy Spirit is praying for you.
- What are you concerned about? Your advocate has your back.
- What are you anxious about? Right now the Holy Spirit is asking God to do what is best for you.

The Holy Spirit is not praying against you. He is not praying for your ill. He is not pleading with God to make you miserable. The Holy Spirit is praying for your good. He is your advocate, not your adversary.

When your prayers are weak, His are strong. When your prayers are confused, His are crystal clear. When your prayers are scattered, His are focused. When your prayers are filled with doubt, His are filled with certainty. When your prayers don't exist, He is persistently and passionately praying for you.

Do you see how involved the Trinity is in your life? The Father made you, the Son redeemed you, and the Holy Spirit saved you, sanctifies you, and helps you in your weaknesses. Nothing falls through the cracks with God. You are not alone in this. Your God has you, your back, your front and everything in between.

The Gospel of the Holy Spirit's Love

Horatius Bonar

Does the Holy Spirit love us? There can be but one answer to this question. Yes! He does.

As truly as the Father loves us, as truly as the Son loves us, so truly does the Spirit love us. That love which we believe to be in God must be the same in each Person of the Godhead, else the Godhead would be divided; one Person at variance with the others, or, at least, less loving than the others: which is impossible.

If there be love in God at all, there must be love in the Spirit. For to Him it is given to carry out in human hearts the purposes of redeeming love, in striving, awakening, drawing, convincing, quickening, comforting; so that it is impossible to suppose that His love can be less warm, less tender, less large, less personal than the love of the Father and the Son.

Perhaps much of our slow progress in the walk of faith is to be traced to our overlooking the love of the Spirit. We do not deal with Him, for strength and advancement, as one who really loves us, and longs to bless us, and delights to help our infirmities (Rom. 8:26).... More childlike confidence in Him and in His love would help us on mightily. Let us not grieve Him, nor vex Him, nor quench Him by our untrustfulness, by disbelieving or doubting the riches of His grace, the abundance of His loving-kindness.

The thoughts of the Spirit are thoughts of love. The apostle uses the words, "the mind of the Spirit," in connection with His gracious intercession (Rom. 8:26–27); and we know that intercession implies love. He thinks of us; and His thoughts are "precious" (Ps. 139:17).

It is the loving Spirit that seals, and witnesses, and indwells, and in-works, and helps, and liberates, and strengthens, and teaches, and baptizes. So that in seeking these blessings we must ever remember that we are dealing with one whose love anticipates our longings, and on whose side there exists no hindrance to our possessing them all.

He has come, in His love, to bind up the broken-hearted. His name is the Comforter, and His consolations are as abundant as they are everlasting. "Comfort you, comfort you my People," are the words which he has written down for every sorrowful one (Isa. 40:1). In all trial, bereavement, pain, sorrow, let us realize the love of the Spirit. That love comes out most brightly and most tenderly in the day of mourning. In the chamber of sickness or of death, let us find strength and peace in the presence, companionship, and sympathy of the gracious Spirit.

He has come, in His love, to build up His own. He seeks to fill, with His holy presence, the soul into which He has come. He wants, not a part of the man, but the whole — body, soul, and spirit — the entire being, that it may be altogether conformed to Himself. He has come to His temples, and His purpose is to make them in reality, what they are in name, the "habitation of God, the temples of the Holy Spirit."[2]

2. Excerpts from http://www.gracegems.org/SERMONS/The%20Holy%20Spirit.htm.

Chapter 10

Anxiety Reliever #6: You Are Going to Get a New Body

Here is how you know you have crossed the line from being young and vibrant to old and rickety. When you watch TV and get annoyed by health product commercials, you are young. When you shush people in the room when health product commercials air, you are old.

Thanks to the Fall, our bodies, like everything else, are under the Curse (Genesis 3:14–19). Unlike evolution, which teaches that things improve with age, the Bible (and simple observation) makes it clear that things fall apart as they get old. And the painful truth is, you and I are falling apart every day.

The older we get, the more we feel the aches of life. Foot arches fall, knees get stiff, joints throb, hair retreats, stomachs bulge, skin sags, organs fail, bumps appear, and energy gets sapped. Our bodies, like the planet, are wearing out like a garment (Hebrews 1:11).

We are all marching, one painful step at a time, toward death. Because each of us has an internal self-preservation mode, we all, to varying degrees fear death. Some carry that fear near the surface and live in dread of taking their last breath. Others don't ever give death a thought — until they have a brush with her.

That is why anxiety reliever number six should bring a smile to your face.

> After a little while the world will no longer see Me, but you will see Me; because **I live, you will live** also. In that day you will know that I am in My Father, and **you in Me**, and I in you (John 14:19–20).

Because you are in Christ and He was raised to life, you are going to be raised to new life also. That's right, you no longer need to fear death.

> Therefore, since the children share in flesh and blood, **He Himself** likewise also partook of the same, that through death He might render powerless him who had the power of death, that is, the devil, and might free those who through **fear of death** were subject to slavery all their lives (Hebrews 2:14–15).

Don't get me wrong — death is still an intruder and none of us look forward to the process of dying, but we no longer need to fear death and the afterlife.

> There is no fear in love; but **perfect love casts out fear**, because fear involves punishment, and the one who fears is not perfected in love (1 John 4:18).

The world fears death because their consciences tell them they are in trouble (Romans 2:15). You and I will not be punished for our sins when we die; Jesus solved that problem for us. We have absolutely nothing to fear about death; we have a Savior who conquered death and rose from the grave. Our Savior will hold our hands as we move from here to the hereafter.

THE BEDROCK MIRACLE

The Resurrection is a sadly overlooked detail of Christian theology; that is a shame because the Resurrection is the bedrock miracle that our faith is built on:

> But if there is no resurrection of the dead, not even Christ has been raised; and **if Christ has not been raised**, then our preaching is vain, your faith also is vain. Moreover we are even found to be false witnesses of God, because we testified against God that He raised Christ, whom He did not raise, if in fact the dead are not raised. For if the dead are not raised, not even Christ has been raised; and if Christ has not been raised, **your faith is worthless**; you are **still in your sins**. Then those also who have fallen asleep in Christ have perished. If we have hoped in Christ in this life only, we are of all men **most to be pitied** (1 Corinthians 15:13–19).

If Jesus is not raised from the dead, then you and I should be more than anxious, we should be downright freaked out. If Jesus didn't rise from the dead, then His sacrifice on the Cross was not acceptable to the Father. If Jesus didn't rise, you and I are still lost in our sins and we are destined for hell.

> But now **Christ has been raised** from the dead, the **first fruits** of those who are asleep (1 Corinthians 15:20).

Jesus is raised from the dead and hundreds of eyewitnesses saw Him (1 Corinthians 15:6). That means there is hope for those who are in Adam; there is a new and better Adam, Jesus Christ. The first man fell, the second man stood. The first man gave into temptation, the second man did not. The first man fell in the Garden, the second man succeeded in the Garden.

> For since by **a man** came death, by **a man** also came the resurrection of the dead. For as **in Adam** all die, so also **in Christ** all will be made alive (1 Corinthians 15:21–22).

If you are in Adam, be anxious, be very anxious. If you are in Christ, there is no need to fear death. Jesus was raised from the dead, and you will be too.

> But each in his own order: Christ the first fruits, after that **those who are Christ's at His coming**, then comes the end, when He hands over the kingdom to the God and Father, when He has abolished all rule and all authority and power (1 Corinthians 15:23–24).

Not only will you be resurrected to eternal life because of Jesus Christ, but you are going to get an eternal body.

> But someone will say, "How are the dead raised? And with **what kind of body** do they come?" . . .
>
> It is sown a perishable body, it is raised an **imperishable body**; it is sown in dishonor, it is raised **in glory**; it is sown in weakness, it is raised in power; it is sown a natural body, it is raised a spiritual body. If there is a natural body, there is also a spiritual body (1 Corinthians 15:35–44).

Eternity is too long for these rickety earthly bodies to last. In order for you to have an eternal body, you need something better than the temporal body you presently inhabit. Because you are in Christ and He was resurrected first, you will be resurrected with a new "spiritual" body that will last for as long as heaven lasts: forever.

That raises a few questions:

1. Will our new bodies be perfect? Define perfect. If you mean the perfect weight, height, and features, I don't think that is much of a concern for God. Your body will be perfect, meaning it will last forever without physical defects.
2. Will I be able to do everything perfectly? I don't think that is what is in view either. Remember, not being able to dunk a basketball is not a sign of imperfection; it is merely a sign of a non-sinful limitation. That means you might still have zero vertical or a 22 handicap.
3. Will I have supernatural abilities? You may get some enhanced features, but you will not be divine. You get to partake of His divine nature, but you and I will not be demi-gods. Our senses will work the way that God designed them, but that doesn't mean we will all be bench-pressing 6,000 pounds.

So what will be so great about being in heaven with our eternal bodies?

> He will **wipe away every tear** from their eyes; and there will **no longer be any death**; there will no longer be any mourning, **or crying, or pain**; the first things have passed away (Revelation 21:4).

What a joy heaven will be, especially compared to earth.

1. You won't experience disease.
2. You won't experience aches and pains.
3. You won't be frustrated because the Curse will be lifted.
4. You will serve the purpose for which you were made.
5. You won't sin. You will only do what is good and right.
6. Death will be dead. You will never have to worry about dying.

> For this perishable must **put on the imperishable**, and this mortal must put on immortality. But when this perishable will have put on the imperishable, and this mortal will have put on immortality, then will come about the saying that is written, "**Death is swallowed up in victory.** O death, where is your

> VICTORY? O DEATH, WHERE IS YOUR STING?" The sting of death is sin, and the power of sin is the law; but thanks be to God, who **gives us the victory** through our Lord Jesus Christ (1 Corinthians 15:53–57).

In other words, you are on the winning side. Death and the devil lose; Jesus wins and we reap the rewards. We do not live in a dualistic universe where God and the devil are duking it out. The devil is God's devil and God wins because He cannot lose. Death will be demolished as sure as you are reading these words (2 Timothy 1:10; Luke 20:36).

Life and death is one of the grand meta-narratives of the Bible. The Curse that was introduced in the first book of the Bible (Genesis 3:17) is destroyed in the last book of the Bible (Revelation 22:3).

The contrast between life and death begins in Genesis, ends in Revelation and is spoken about all throughout the Bible (Matthew 15:25–26; John 3:16, 3:36, 6:40; Acts 2:29–34; Romans 5:12; 1 Thessalonians 4:13–14; 1 John 5:12; Revelation 22:1–5, plus dozens and dozens more).

- God created the world and all of the life in it (Genesis 1–2).
- Man sinned and introduced death (Genesis 3).
- God immediately promised to send One who would destroy death (Genesis 3:14–15).
- The entire Old Testament foreshadows the coming of the death destroyer.
- Jesus arrives, announcing that anyone who believes in Him will not perish but have everlasting life (John 3:16).
- The Book of Acts describes how the disciples brought this message of life to the world.
- The Epistles give detailed instructions to the early church about living as inheritors of everlasting life.
- The Book of Revelation describes how the devil and death will be defeated and we will reign with God forever in the new heavens and the new earth.

Did you catch that? You get to reign with Jesus Christ.

> It is a trustworthy statement:
> For if we died with Him, we will also **live with Him**;

> If we endure, we will also **reign with Him**;
> If we deny Him, He also will deny us;
> If we are faithless, He remains faithful, for He cannot deny Himself (2 Timothy 2:11–13).

Your position in Adam = enemy of God. Your position in Christ = co-reigner with God.

> He who overcomes, and he who keeps My deeds until the end, TO HIM **I WILL GIVE AUTHORITY OVER THE NATIONS**; AND HE SHALL **RULE THEM** WITH A ROD OF IRON, AS THE VESSELS OF THE POTTER ARE BROKEN TO PIECES, as I also have received *authority* from My Father; and I will **give him the morning star**. He who has an ear, let him hear what the Spirit says to the churches (Revelation 2:26–29).

If you have ever wondered what you will be doing for eternity, those verses give us a clue: you will be reigning over the universe with Jesus Christ. You will not be omnipotent and omnipresent, but you will have a job overseeing His creation.

I suspect you will be doing something you love, something that He has gifted you for. Best of all, while you are busy working, it will be work without hassles, frustration, and thorns. You won't be frustrated by dropped calls, slow wi-fi, or incompetent workers. You will feel the sense of accomplishment that comes from work, without the annoyances.

What Else Will We Do?

Randy Alcorn asks a great heavenly question, "Why would we do anything less in heaven (which is greater) than we do now on earth (which is the lesser)? There is no reason to believe that we will not have arts, sciences, music, paintings, humor, laughter, sports, accomplishments, pottery, food, hobbies, and every other good thing we currently enjoy.

Will we spend time worshiping Jesus? Of course, but the whole of our existence will be dedicated to worshiping Jesus, even when we are not singing to Him. Everything we do, eat, hear, or smell will be with the thought, "Jesus made this." We will live life in heaven the way we are supposed to be living on earth.

Solomon described our current life as "vanity of vanities" (Ecclesiastes 1:2). The wisest man in the world said that everything we do is worthless: work, eating, knowledge, intimacy, family, everything. It is all worthless without the last two verses of the book.

> The conclusion, when all has been heard, is: fear God and keep His commandments, because this applies to every person. For God will bring **every act to judgment**, everything which is hidden, whether it is good or evil (Ecclesiastes 12:13–14).

Everything we do in this life is absolutely worthless unless we are doing it for the Lord. Unless we work for Him, play for Him, sing for Him, raise our kids for Him, eat for Him, volunteer for Him, then we are doing worthless things. But if we are doing all things for His glory (1 Corinthians 10:31), then our labors have eternal value and a sense of fulfillment.

Our problem (among others) is that you and I tend to enjoy His gifts without recognizing the giver. When we get to heaven, we will experience everything we do with God in mind. That is why heaven will be so much better than earth. You and I will live in constant recognition that it is God Himself who allows us to live and move and have our being (Acts 17:28).

More than that, we will spend eternity getting to know and enjoy the best thing there is: God Himself. This will be the most profound experience we can imagine. You get to spend forever learning new and amazing things about the most amazing entity of all — your Maker.

If I told you that you have to go to Chick-fil-A and drink a large cookies and cream milkshake, you probably wouldn't think that was much of a command. In fact, you would likely think of it as a delight. Needless to say, God is more profound than a malt.

This may sound a little shocking to you, but the nearest thing we have on earth to help us understand how amazing heaven will be is intimacy between a man and wife.

How Euphoric Will Heaven Be?

It is a shame that we Christians talk about intimacy like it is a dirty activity; it is not. In fact, God told Adam and Eve to be fruitful and multiply BEFORE the Fall (Genesis 1:28). There is only one way to multiply: intimacy. Sex between a husband and wife is not in and of itself dirty; it is sin that causes us to not trust one another and cover our nudity and think sex is a shameful thing (Genesis 3:7). If it weren't for sin, intimacy would not be sinful, shameful, dirty, or profane.

Intimacy between a husband and wife is a physical picture of a greater spiritual reality. Paul tells us what that reality is when he tells us that the male-female covenant union between a man and woman is a picture of the relationship between Jesus and His Church (Ephesians 5:32).

Marriage, and the intimacy which is the zenith of that relationship, signifies the intimacy that should exist between Jesus and His Church. That intimacy will be fully known when we are in heaven and we see Him as He is (1 John 3:2). When a man and woman physically join together, it is a foreshadowing of the intimacy we will enjoy with God in heaven. No, we will not be sexual with God, but sex is a foretaste of the experience of fully knowing God in an intimate, non-sexual way.

To put it bluntly: if you think sex is amazing on earth, wait until you are in a glorified, right relationship with the Creator of the universe. Sex will pale in comparison to the joy of being with your God without any of the effects of sin. To be clear, our relationship with God is not, and never will be, sexual in nature. But sex is indeed a physical picture of a spiritual reality.

You will spend eternity getting to know the One who transcends any earthly delight (including sex between a husband and wife). You will forever know and be known by the One who knows every single detail about you.

New Name

Imagine for a moment that there is someone who knows you better than you know yourself. This person knows your hopes, your fears, your anxious thoughts, your hurts, your sorrows, your joys, your favorite things, and your worst nightmares. This imaginary person understands who you are better than you do.

Now, imagine this person with intimate knowledge of you decided to give you a new name that captures the very essence of you. Not even you can figure out what that essence is because your sin clouds even your judgment of yourself. But this person's judgment isn't clouded. This person has the ability to give you a name that causes you, for the first time ever, to say, "Yes! That is exactly who I am."

You don't have to imagine. God is the One who knows you intimately, and He promises to give you that new name when you are in heaven.

> He who has an ear, let him hear what the Spirit says to the churches. To him **who overcomes**, to him I will give some of the hidden manna, and I will give him a white stone, and **a new name written on the stone** which **no one knows** but he who receives it (Revelation 2:17–18).

God is going to give you a stone with your new name that causes you to say, "Yes, that is exactly who I am. I have never been able to articulate how I feel about myself. Finally, I am known for who I am and what I am. And I don't have to feel ashamed." That should give you a small taste of the joys of knowing God and being known by your God. That is why you and I will spend eternity praising Him in everything we do.

- You will play sports with total enjoyment in recognition that it was provided by the One who knows you and loves you more than anyone ever has.
- You will not just thank God before you dine at His table (Matthew 8:11), you will enjoy every chew of every bite of every item that He serves you on your plate.
- You will interact with other members of the Kingdom without fear of shame, retribution, or bullying. There are no cliques in heaven.
- You will understand righteousness and justice and goodness so profoundly that you will not weep over those who are in hell (Revelation 19:3).
- When you remember life on earth (there is no reason to believe you will be mind-swiped as you enter heaven), you will not weep over calamities, because you will fully grasp that every detail of your life was lovingly planned by your gracious Heavenly Father.
- You will worship Him without mental distractions because your thinking will finally be right. Even if God doesn't give you better pitch, you will joyfully sing at the top of your lungs without worrying about the person standing in front of you.

Best of all, this is all free. Free. Free. Free.

> For the wages of sin is death, but the **free gift** of God is **eternal life** in Christ Jesus our Lord (Romans 6:23).

You and I have earned death for ourselves; Jesus Christ purchased eternal life for us. Jesus gets our sin; we get His righteousness. We earned hell and Jesus bought us heaven. You and I should get wrath, but Jesus bought us paradise. We should be cast under the sovereign foot of God; instead, He invites us to reign with Him.

That is why Paul finished his treatise on heaven in 1 Corinthians 15 with this conclusion:

> Therefore, my beloved brethren, **be steadfast, immovable**, always abounding in the work of the Lord, knowing that your toil is not in vain **in the Lord** (1 Corinthians 15:58).

The knowledge that we die and immediately go to be with Him forever (2 Corinthians 5:8; Hebrews 9:27) should cause us to live steadfastly while we remain on earth. Thoughts of being in heaven with an eternal body should steady your emotions. Heavenly thoughts will always trump earthly woes.

You don't even have to worry about the devil — he is a vanquished foe who is going to spend eternity locked up in hell while you are rejoicing in heaven (2 Peter 2:4; Revelation 20:2–3).

- You don't have to worry about death because it will be destroyed (1 Corinthians 15:26).
- You don't have to worry about illness because it will be vanquished (Revelation 21:4).
- You don't have to worry about your worrying because all worries will be gone forever (Revelation 21:4).

We are merely exiles here (Hebrews 11:13), but on a day of God's own choosing, He will deliver you from this body of death (Romans 7:24) and you will spend eternity with your eternal body enjoying your God so profoundly that the delights of this life will seem like trifles by comparison.

Do you fear death? You don't have to.

> Truly, truly, I say to you, he who hears My word, and believes Him who sent Me, has eternal life, and does not come into judgment, but has **passed out of death into life** (John 5:24).

Are you feeling miserable because of the aches in your body? Think about eternal life with your new pain-free body.

> For I consider that the sufferings of this present time are **not worthy to be compared** with the glory that is to be revealed to us (Romans 8:18).

Jesus asked Martha a profound question that He asks you today:

> Jesus said to her, "I am the **resurrection and the life**; he who believes in Me will live even if he dies, and everyone who lives and believes in Me **will never die**. Do you believe this?" (John 11:25–26).

If you believe that Jesus is the resurrection and the life, then you are going to be resurrected with an everlasting body to enjoy God forever and ever and ever (John 14:19). Ponder that the next time you are anxious and let that truth drive your anxiety away.

The Earthly and the Heavenly

"We shall be like Him." — **I John 3:2**.

"We shall be like Him." **In what?** In all things in which it is possible for the created to be like Jesus. Even now are we the sons of God, but then shall we really be, in all respects, soul and body, what we are now only by title.

"We shall be like Him." **Who?** Those who are His! Those who have received this crucified and risen Christ as their Lord and God. He who believes on Him now, shall wear His likeness when He appears.

"We shall be like Him." **How long?** Forever! No losing of that likeness in the process of the ages. No feature nor line of a feature becoming effaced — but ever deepening and deepening — likeness to Jesus becoming greater — perfection becoming more perfect — throughout eternity.

In a dying world like ours, it soothes and cheers to think of resurrection. Yes, resurrection! How bright the thought and dear the word! Resurrection will complete the conformity to the image of the heavenly. Perfection of body as well as soul! No suffering and no sinning! Is not this hope glorious? Does it not (1) stimulate, (2) sanctify, (3) comfort? Should it not quicken prayer and watchfulness?

Blessed thought! Perfection in — wisdom, light, holiness, love, and glory! No more dimness, or cloud, or vagueness, or guessing, or groping. All shall be fullness, and perfection, and glory forever!

What blessedness is in this prospect! How it cheers! How it makes us content with weakness and imperfection for a time! How it quickens us to press forward to the perfect and the glorious![1]

1. Excerpts from http://gracegems.org/19/r32.htm.

Chapter 11

Anxiety Reliever #7: You Have Real Peace

The world promises peace in many forms:

- Self-esteem
- Alcohol
- Medication
- Vacations
- Cabins
- Education
- Mind training
- Long walks
- Sex
- Drugs
- Meditation
- Cruises
- Relationships
- Careers
- False religions
- Naps

Leave it to Jesus to crash all of those worldly promises with anxiety reliever number seven.

> **Peace I leave with you**; My peace I give to you; not as the world gives do I give to you. Do not let your heart be troubled, nor let it be fearful (John 14:27).

Bye-bye, Oprah. So long, psychiatric professionals. Adios, Wall Street. Sayonara, Eastern religions. Jesus slams the door on every offer of worldly peace and stakes His un-politically correct claim, "Any method for peace besides Me, is false."

- Secular psychiatry is false
- Mindfulness is false
- Binge drinking is false
- Buddhism is false
- Hinduism is false
- Meditation is false
- Hooking up is false
- Yoga is false

If you hear an ad that offers peace through any mechanism besides Jesus, it is a lie. The world can bring happiness, fun, excitement, laughter, amusement, and a hangover, but it cannot give you true peace. Only Jesus can do that.

The world can offer external pleasantries (smells, tastes, sounds, sights), but external niceties cannot change your internal thinking. If you are miserable in a 1,500-square-foot home, you will not have more peace in a 4,500-square-foot home. You will simply have more rooms to be unhappy in.

If you are anxious about having $5,000 in monthly expenses, you will still be anxious if you only have $2,000 in monthly bills. If you are sad because your closet isn't filled with designer clothes, you might look better if you buy some Gucci, but you will not be happier. Anxiety is not an external issue. Inner peace does not come from external baubles.

Don't get me wrong, God has provided many fine things for us to enjoy, but those enjoyments have limitations. At best, they are fleeting; only the peace that comes from Jesus brings true contentment.

Shalom

Jesus is the Prince of Peace who died in the city of peace that you and I might have peace with God through faith in Him.

> Therefore, having been justified by faith, we have **peace with God through our Lord Jesus Christ**, through whom also we have obtained our introduction by faith into this grace in which we stand; and we exult in hope of the glory of God (Romans 5:1–2).

Peace, true peace, only comes from being in a right relationship with our Maker. Only when we have been "justified by faith," do we have peace.

If we are not transferred from Adam to Christ, our lives will be miserable. You see, we have this little mechanism that is standard factory equipment built into every human brain: the conscience, which either convicts or defends us (Romans 2:15). When we listen rightly to our consciences, we hear it scream, "Condemned."

Because of our sin and rebellion, our consciences are like a black cloud hanging over our heads. We feel the weight of our sin and we sense echoes of judgment day. The unregenerate man or woman can never sleep soundly with strains of "Guilty" playing in their heads. A man on death row may enjoy bites of his last meal, but each morsel is swallowed hard with the knowledge of imminent death.

You are not on death row. Your conscience is clean. Your crimes are erased from the books. More than that, you are not merely a forgiven criminal, you are now the righteousness of God (2 Corinthians 5:21). You have been justified by faith and have peace with God through our Lord Jesus Christ (Romans 5:1).

No justification, no peace. Because of justification, our single biggest problem has been solved; we do not have to face the furious wrath of God. But justification is even greater than forgiveness. Justification grants us righteousness.

Think of it like this: you owe an earthly judge five million dollars, which you do not have. One day, you open the mail to discover that not only has someone paid your entire fine, but this benevolent man also put an extra fifty million into your bank account.

That is what Jesus Christ has done for you. He not only died to forgive your sins, but He also lived a perfectly righteous life and credited all of that merit to your account. That means you are not just seen by God as forgiven, you are seen as righteous when you are justified through faith in Christ.

> He made Him who knew no sin to be sin on our behalf, so that we might become **the righteousness of God in Him** (2 Corinthians 5:21).

You, a wretched, vile, fist-shaking sinner, were on a collision course with the just Judge of all the earth. You were scheduled to meet the One who promises to grind guilty sinners to powder (Matthew 21:44). You were without excuse, without hope, and without a defense attorney.

But now you have an advocate — Jesus, the Righteous (1 John 2:1). Not only did Jesus take the punishment for the sins you have committed against God, but He also lived a perfect life of righteousness and He applies His goodness to your account.

Your biggest problem in life is officially solved because of Jesus Christ. If the Son has set you free, then you are free indeed (John 8:36).

- Would you be concerned about a sliver in your finger if you just learned that your cancer was benign?

- Would you fret about owing someone $5.00 if you had a million dollars in your bank account?
- If you just missed a head-on collision with a semi, would you be upset about a tiny ding from a pebble that flew up and glanced your fender?
- If an airplane just dropped a bomb on your front yard but it didn't detonate, would you complain that your teenager didn't cut the lawn?
- Because you are in Jesus Christ, God's wrath against you no longer exists. Nothing in life should now cause you to worry about anything ever again. Anything we worry about is downright silly when we remember that our biggest worry has been dealt with.

That is why peace and salvation are inextricably linked. The knowledge that we have peace with the just Judge of all the earth allows us to remain calm while the world is falling apart. The worst problem you can imagine pales in comparison to the problem you used to have with God. That knowledge should change our tune from "Woe is me" to "Praise God from whom all blessings flow."

- The stock market crashed and I lost my fortune; but I am not going to be sent to hell.
- We lost the election; but the King of the universe has elected me to salvation.
- The enemy is at the gate; but God, the consuming fire, is no longer my adversary.
- My child is a prodigal; but I have been found by a loving Father.
- I just got terminated; but God is not going to condemn me to a lake of fire.

Name the worst tragedy that can befall you and it is a pittance compared to facing the fierce wrath of an angry God. This is not to suggest that your problems are not real; life is hard. Nevertheless, knowing that your earthly problems are no match for the eternal problem that has been solved for you will bring you peace. When the world is going bonkers, we can still have peace because we have the most important and precious thing in the world: forgiveness of sins. Peace and salvation go hand in hand. Jesus repeats this theme regularly. Like, a lot.

The Beatitudes

Liberal theologians claim the Beatitudes are to be interpreted like this: "If you do the things Jesus lists, then you will be blessed." Jesus was teaching the exact opposite; the people who are redeemed are the blessed ones. He reiterates that with each of the nine beatitudes; here are just two examples of happy, redeemed people.

> Blessed are the **poor in spirit**, for theirs is the kingdom of heaven (Matthew 5:3).

Jesus is basically saying, "The blessed person is the one who knows he is going to heaven because he has been saved by being totally broken over sin."

> Blessed are those who mourn, for they shall be comforted (Matthew 5:4).

The one who mourned over sin and got saved is the one who will have every tear wiped away in heaven (Revelation 21:4). That knowledge makes the redeemed very happy. Jesus repeats that idea seven more times. His point? If you are saved, you will be blessed/happy. Salvation and peace go hand in hand.

Living Water

Without physical water, humans perish temporally. Without spiritual water, humans perish eternally. Thankfully, we have living water.

> Now on the last day, the great day of the feast, Jesus stood and cried out, saying, "If anyone is **thirsty**, let him **come to Me and drink**. He who believes in Me, as the Scripture said, 'From his innermost being will flow rivers of living water' " (John 7:37–38).

In the Old Testament, God provided water to temporarily satisfy the physical thirst of the parched Jews wandering in the wilderness. Jesus announced that He is the free, living water who will eternally satisfy our spiritual thirst. Jesus is our living water that rescues us from the unquenchable physical thirst we deserve to experience in hell (Luke 16:24).

Eternally damned sinners long for a single drop of water to quench their raging thirst. Because you have consumed the living water, you will never experience that torment. Peace and salvation go hand in hand.

Bread

When the Jews were wandering in the wilderness, God provided life-sustaining bread. This too was a picture of Jesus.

> Jesus said to them, "I am the **bread of life**; he who comes to Me will **not hunger**, and he who believes in Me will never thirst" (John 6:35).

Undoubtedly Jesus was referring to Isaiah 55:

> Ho! Every one who thirsts, come to the waters;
> And you who have **no money** come, buy and eat.
> Come, buy wine and milk
> Without money and **without cost**.
> Why do you spend money for what is **not bread**,
> And your wages for what does not satisfy?
> Listen carefully to Me, and eat what is good,
> And delight yourself in abundance.
> Incline your ear and come to Me.
> Listen, that **you may live**;
> And I will make an everlasting covenant with you,
> According to the faithful mercies shown to David (Isaiah 55:1–3).

Jesus revealed that the Old Testament manna was actually a fuzzy picture of Himself. Manna temporarily satisfied a physical need; Jesus forever satisfies our spiritual need. Every time your stomach rumbles, you should pause and remember that your spiritual hunger has been forever satisfied in Jesus. Peace and salvation go hand in hand.

Because we have peace with God through our salvation, there is now no excuse for being anxious. You and I experience anxiety when we take our eyes off of our heavenly peace and look to worldly things to bring us serenity. This is a classic and easy error to make.

Lies, Lies, Lies

The world we live in has a "system." The world system is not the world itself; instead it is a system of worldviews, false religions, and false ideologies that lead people astray (2 Corinthians 10:5). False world systems take many forms, like: secular humanism, godlessness, human reason, progressivism, worldly marketing, and any thing or one that sets itself up against the truth.

The world system wants you to believe, think, and act in every way that is contrary to God; and it is very good at what it does. The world system has tangled billions in its web because the world system is a lot like Charlie Brown's sister.

The Bible describes sin as deceitful (Hebrews 3:13). The chief deceiver, the devil, is the father of lies (John 8:44); and his modus operandi to lead humans into temptation is lying. The devil is in control of the world system (John 12:31; Ephesians 2:2, 6:12; 1 John 5:19). Therefore, the world system lies.

Here are some of the lies that the devil-controlled world system tries to tempt you with:

- Buy a big house and you will be happy.
- Move into that neighborhood and you will be content.
- Own that wardrobe and others will like you.
- Acquire that job and you will be respected.
- Save so much money and you will be safe.
- Sacrifice your family for work and you will be satisfied.

On and on the lies go, and we keep buying them. We are like Charlie Brown who continues to believe Lucy's lie: "Go ahead, Charlie Brown, I will hold the football this time. Kick it." And just like Charlie, we end up on our backs wondering why we keep buying the lie.

> **Do not love the world** nor the things in the world. If anyone loves the world, the love of the Father is not in him. For all that is in the world, the **lust of the flesh** and the **lust of the eyes** and the boastful pride of life, is **not from the Father**, but is from the world. The world is passing away, and also its lusts; but the one who does the will of God lives forever (1 John 2:15–17).

If you are lacking peace, you are probably buying the lies of the world system. If you are lacking peace, you are looking for peace in all the wrong places. If you are lacking peace, you are not appropriating the true peace that Jesus alone gives.

Why We Fight

Would you like to know why we don't have peace with people? The Bible asks and answers that elusive question.

> What is the **source of quarrels** and conflicts among you? Is not the source your pleasures that wage war in your members? You lust and do not have; so you commit murder. You are envious and cannot obtain; so you **fight and quarrel** (James 4:1–2).

When you and I need something and our desire is thwarted, we go to war against the person who is hindering our satisfaction. We do this all the time.

- You and I want to watch the football game, but the kids keep interrupting. How do we respond? We go to war and yell at them.
- You and I want our spouse to look or act a certain way, but they don't. How do we respond? We fight and quarrel.
- You and I want to get to church on time, but a family member takes too long to get ready. How do we respond? We murder them with our words. "Get in the van, you ungrateful brat, I don't want to be late for church."

As if that isn't painful enough to read, James goes a step further and scolds us by diagnosing our hearts:

> You **adulteresses**, do you not know that **friendship with the world** is hostility toward God? Therefore whoever wishes to be a friend of the world makes himself **an enemy of God** (James 4:4).

Ouch, there it is again. When you and I seek satisfaction in worldly things, we are acting like enemies of God. No wonder worldly things don't satisfy. No wonder we don't have peace. When we love the things of this world, we are not only not loving God, we act like an enemy.

Some Christian marriage books tell you to have peace by scratching your spouse's back and he/she will scratch yours. If you figure out your spouse's love needs and satisfy them, then he/she will figure out and satisfy your needs. That is not Christian and that will not bring peace.

1. Your sinful back scratcher will fail you and not scratch you when and how you need it, and you will continue to go to war.

2. The Christian faith is not a "quid pro quo" kind of faith. Christians should serve one another because we have been served by our Master.

How do we stop fights and have peace? By remembering that peace and salvation go hand in hand. Jesus did not wait for you to do something for Him before He died for you. Jesus died for you while you were sinning, not scratching His back.

> For while we were still **helpless**, at the right time Christ died for the ungodly. For one will hardly die for a righteous man; though perhaps for the good man someone would dare even to die. But God demonstrates His own love toward us, in that **while we were yet sinners**, Christ died for us. Much more then, having now been justified by His blood, we shall be saved from the **wrath of God** through Him. For if while we were **enemies** we were **reconciled** to God through the death of His Son, **much more**, having been reconciled, we shall be saved by His life. And not only this, but we also **exult in God** through our Lord Jesus Christ, through whom we have now received the **reconciliation** (Romans 5:6–11).

Jesus did not wait for you to do something good for Him before He did something amazing for you. Dwelling on that knowledge frees you to love people even if they never return the kindness. Christianity says, "All of my needs have been met by Jesus Christ. I have no needs." That knowledge means you can now love people without needing them to return the favor.

Because self-sacrificial agape love is the highest form of love, you will never agape love your family until you don't need your family. When you need your family then you will either do things to get things in return, or you will be annoyed when you do more for them than they do for you.

Christianity is not about keeping score. Knowing that my score has been settled by Jesus, I no longer keep track of who does what for whom. Jesus loved us totally when we offered Him nothing. I don't need anyone to love me because I am loved sufficiently by my God. Now I am free to love others even when they offer me nothing.

All of our needs have been met in Jesus Christ. I don't need anyone for anything because I have everything I need in Jesus. Now I can love others because I want to, not because I have to. While it is perfectly fine to want a happy spouse and well-behaved children, the moment we need them, we will go to war.

Salvation and peace go hand in hand. The Prince of Peace brings His peace to your heart, mind, emotions, family, and life when you ponder the peace that you now have because of Him.

The next time you are inclined to worry or fight about anything, stop and ponder your salvation. Think about the bullet Jesus allows you to dodge. Consider what your life would be like if you were still on a highway to hell. Jesus signed the greatest peace treaty ever with His blood for you. Let that give you the perspective you need to say, "The Lord is my shepherd, I shall not want."

Pierced!

James Smith, 1860

"He was **pierced** for our transgressions, He was ***crushed*** for our iniquities; the punishment that brought us **peace** was upon Him, and by His wounds we are healed!" Isaiah 53:5.

If we would **enjoy peace**, grow in grace, and walk with God — there is *one object* on which the *eye of the mind* should be constantly fixed. Therefore it is written, as the language of our crucified Lord, "They shall look upon Me whom they have pierced!" Zechariah 12:10.

Pierced! Who pierced Him? We did — and pierced Him to the heart! Nor were we satisfied with piercing Him once — our unbelief pierces Him; our ingratitude pierces Him; the coldness of our love pierces Him; our forgetfulness pierces Him; our preferring the world to Him pierces Him; our disobedience to His Word pierces Him; and our doubting of His love pierces Him!

It was *WE* who pierced Him on Calvary! We put the *nails* and the *hammer* into the hands of the executioners! We put the *spear* into the hand of the Roman soldier! Yes, it was we who gathered the *thorns*, picked out the sharpest, formed them into a mock crown, thrust it on His head, and with the staff beat the thorns into His temples!

See, see, there He hangs! Pierced in His head, hands, feet, and side — pierced **for** us — pierced **by** us! Look, my soul, at *the pierced One!*

God's holy Son hangs on that cross!

O my soul, look at Jesus! He is your Substitute. He is there *for you!* He is suffering death *for you!* He is bearing *the desert of your sins* in His body on the tree! He is enduring your curse, being made accursed for you!

O Savior, was ever any *love*, was ever any *agony*, was ever any *death* — like Yours!

Look, my soul, look to Jesus, the pierced One! Look, and **mourn** — because *your* sins degraded, disgraced, and put Him to grief! Look, and **rejoice**, for you shall have dignity — by His degradation, honor — by His disgrace, and life — by His death!

Look, and be **sorry** that you have ever sinned, and so caused Jesus to suffer! Look, and **rejoice** that you shall live forever to glorify and praise His name!

O my soul, Jesus was wounded for *your* transgressions, and bruised for *your* iniquities! His *blood* has made your peace with God, His *righteousness* gives you a title to eternal life, and His *death* delivers you from dying!

I fix my eye intently on Jesus on the *Hill Calvary*, and marking all His tears, wounds, and agonies — I feel that *I was the cause of all*. I myself did it! Yes, I MYSELF bruised Him, scourged Him, spit on Him, crowned Him with thorns, smote Him with the fist, and nailed Him to the cursed tree! *I inflicted it all.*

Yet, O wonder of wonders! I derive pardon, holiness, and eternal life from it! And I have peace.[1]

1. Excerpts from http://www.gracegems.org/2016/03/pierced.html.

Chapter 12

Anxiety Reliever #8: You Have an Avenger

Kids can be so cruel. Adults aren't much better. If you were bullied as a child or wounded as an adult, Jesus has a great anxiety reliever for you.

> You heard that I said to you, "I go away, and **I will come to you**." If you loved Me, you would have rejoiced because I go to the Father, for the Father is greater than I (John 14:28).

Anxiety reliever number eight is: Judgment Day.

> It is only just for God to repay with affliction **those who afflict you**, and to give relief to you who are afflicted and to us as well when the Lord **Jesus will be revealed** from heaven with His mighty angels in flaming fire, dealing out **retribution** to those who do not know God and to those who do not obey the gospel of our Lord Jesus. These will pay the penalty of **eternal destruction**, away from the presence of the Lord and from the glory of His power, **when He comes** to be glorified in His saints on that day, and to be marveled at among all who have believed (2 Thessalonians 1:6–10).

You have an Avenger and His name is Jesus Christ (1 Thessalonians 4:6). He will seek, find, and destroy every unredeemed sinner who has ever sinned against you when He returns to judge the living and the dead. Your Avenger will utterly crush your enemies. Whatever awful deed has been done to you, the Lion of Judah will pursue your nemesis and utterly demolish them as He casts your offenders into an eternal Lake of Sulfur.

Your enemies will beg for the mountains to fall on them when Warrior Jesus returns on a stallion to wage war against the unredeemed.

> I looked when He broke the sixth seal, and there was a **great earthquake**; and the sun became black as sackcloth made of hair, and the whole moon became like blood; and the **stars of the sky fell** to the earth, as a fig tree casts its unripe figs when shaken by a great wind. The sky was split apart like a scroll when it is rolled up, and every mountain and island were moved out of their places. Then the **kings** of the earth and the **great men** and the **commanders** and the **rich** and the **strong** and **every slave and free man** hid themselves in the caves and among the rocks of the mountains; and they said to the mountains and to the rocks, "**Fall on us** and **hide us** from the presence of Him who sits on the throne, and from the **wrath of the Lamb**; for the great day of their wrath has come, and who is able to stand" (Revelation 6:12–17)?

Do you really think you can do a better job of dealing with your enemies than that? God's justice is so thorough that no man, regardless of status, will escape. The Lord's justice is total, unremitting, and unbearable.

- Who has been troubling you? You have an Avenger.
- Who has caused you grief? Your Avenger will punish that person on your behalf.
- Who has done wicked things to you? You will receive justice as your God grinds your enemy to powder (Matthew 21:44).

Were you molested as a child and no one believed you when you reached out for help? Your abuser stands no chance against King Jesus. Were you jilted or ripped off as an adult? Jesus is going to engage in a seek, find, and destroy mission against those who have wounded you.

- Why are you harboring vengeance when that is your Avenger's job? He will do it better than anything you could ever imagine.
- Why do you still hold a grudge when your Avenger has written their sinful deed in His book of remembrance (Revelation 20:12–15)?
- Why are you bitter toward people who have wounded you when the Captain of your salvation is going to war against unregenerate sinners?

You do not need to hold onto your vengeful feelings for two reasons: your vengeance is sinful and God's is not. Besides, He is going to do a much better job of avenging the sins committed against you than you ever could.

Big Sins, Big Punishment

This is a truly wicked world. People do atrocious things. Perhaps something appalling has been done to you.

- Perhaps you have been sexually abused
- Perhaps somebody took the life of a loved one
- Perhaps somebody pressured you to abort your child
- Perhaps you have been debilitated because of a drunk driver

Rest assured, my dear friend, your God saw it and tolerated it, but He has not forgotten it. He recorded those events in a book (Revelation 20:12) and He will slay your abuser. He will extend no mercy and He will grant no reprieve from the unrelenting punishment He will dole out on them.

You do not need to harbor pain, bitterness, grief, sorrow, anger, or vengeance. You do not need to remember that awful sin any more.

> **Never** take your own revenge, beloved, but leave room for the wrath of God, for it is written, "**VENGEANCE IS MINE**, I WILL REPAY," SAYS THE LORD (Romans 12:19).

This is going to sound radical, but leaving vengeance to God allows you to obey the command to love your enemies (Matthew 5:44).

> BUT IF YOUR ENEMY IS HUNGRY, FEED HIM, AND IF HE IS THIRSTY, GIVE HIM A DRINK; FOR IN SO DOING YOU WILL HEAP BURNING COALS ON HIS HEAD." Do not be overcome by evil, but **overcome evil with good** (Romans 12:20–21).

That is a profound command: overcome evil with good. We are not commanded to pretend evil never happens, we are called to counter wickedness with kindness. How can we possibly do that?

Healing with Judgment Day in Mind

Step #1: Your desire for vengeance can be mortified when you remember that Jesus is going to avenge the sins committed against you.

Step #2: You can begin to heal when you remember that God will avenge the abuse you have received.

Step #3: You can grow in gratitude to God for sending Jesus to receive the dreadful punishment you deserve for the sins you have committed against other people.

Step #4: If you continue to remember Judgment Day, you will begin to quickly respond to evil with love.

Step #5: The deeper you grow in your knowledge of the great and dreadful day of the Lord, the more you will actually begin to pray that your enemies get saved so they will not have to:

> . . . drink of the wine of the **wrath** of God, which is mixed in **full strength** in the cup of His anger; and he will be **tormented** with fire and brimstone in the presence of the holy angels and in the presence of the Lamb. And the smoke of their torment goes up forever and ever; they have no rest day and night (Revelation 14:10–11).

As you grow in gratitude to Jesus for drinking your cup of wrath down to the dregs, you will begin to desire that even the worst people in your life will escape God's fury.

> And I saw heaven opened, and behold, a white horse, and He who sat on it is called Faithful and True, and in righteousness He judges and wages war. His **eyes are a flame of fire**, and on His head are many diadems; and He has a name written on Him which no one knows except Himself. He is clothed with a **robe dipped in blood**, and His name is called The Word of God. And the armies which are in heaven, clothed in fine linen, white and clean, were following Him on white horses. From His mouth comes a **sharp sword**, so that with it He may strike down the nations, and He will rule them with a **rod of iron**; and He treads the wine press of the **fierce wrath of God**, the Almighty. And on His robe and on His thigh He has a name written, "KING OF KINGS, AND LORD OF LORDS" (Revelation 19:11–16).

See the eyes of the ungodly as they see the King of kings wearing a robe dipped in blood racing toward them.

Hear the sword of Jesus being drawn from its sheath.

Stand in horror as the Lord of lords hurls your foes into outer darkness.

When we earnestly ponder the fate of the ungodly, that fearful knowledge will change our hearts from anger, bitterness, and revenge to concern, compassion, and even love.

- Can you hear the cries of the ungodly in hell?
- Can you smell the smoke of their torment?
- Can you see them in utter despair that never ends?

When you change your calendar at the New Year and remember that the souls in hell are never one day closer to their release, you will grow in earnest concern for the sake of the lost. Remember, God does not cast people to hell with the glee of a child headed to a circus. God sends people to hell because it is just and right, not because He takes pleasure in the death of the wicked (Ezekiel 18:23). The more our thinking is transformed into God's thinking, we won't either.

You Escaped Judgment Day

What you are about to read is not easy; this is top-shelf Christianity. This is a hard concept but it is your path to not only coping with your pain, but also how you can actually love your perpetrators. Your path to healing means focusing on this verse:

> But God demonstrates His own love toward us, in that while we were **yet sinners**, Christ died for us. Much more then, having now been justified by His blood, we shall be saved from the **wrath of God** through Him. For if while we were **enemies** we were reconciled to God through the death of His Son, much more, having been reconciled, we shall be saved by His life (Romans 5:8–10).

Our path to peace starts by remembering that Jesus loved us while we were racing headlong to hell. We have escaped the awesome day of the Lord because Jesus loved us.

We have committed more and greater sins against our Savior than anything that has ever been done to us. As we remember that Jesus loved us while we were happily committing crimes against Him, it becomes increasingly difficult to not forgive people who have done less to us than we did to Him (Matthew 18:21–35).

Think how Jesus experienced the eternal thrashing you deserve so that you could be set free, forgiven and adopted as a child of God. The more you grow in your knowledge of God's great love for you, the more you will actually be able to love your enemies.

Perhaps you think that is utterly impossible. It may feel that way now, but remember, you have the same Holy Spirit in you that allowed Jesus to love the friend who betrayed Him. When Jesus announced that one of the disciples would betray Him, nobody piped up and said, "It's Judas!" That is because Jesus loved Judas the same way He loved the disciples who were faithful.

You can forgive your enemies by the power of the same Holy Spirit that allowed Jesus to pray for forgiveness for those who mocked, beat, spat, and nailed His hands and feet to a cross (Luke 23:34).

You Have Been Wounded Profoundly

It is a crushing reality that wicked atrocities happen frequently. Children get abused and adults get violated daily. When something dirty has been done to us, we feel a level of shame that is almost unspeakable.

- Perhaps you have been living your Christian life lacking joy because of wicked sin that was perpetrated against you.
- Perhaps you feel like a second-class Christian because of that horrific event.
- Perhaps you are frightened that someone might find out about the horrific things that were done to you and you will be a shamed Christian outcast.
- Perhaps you feel like you have been forgiven for all of your sins, but God doesn't actually love someone as tainted as you.
- Perhaps you feel repulsed by yourself because you think there may have been moments that you actually enjoyed the sin being committed against you.

May I lovingly but firmly tell you, your thinking is wrong. This is a time when facts need to speak to your feelings. Here are the facts; there are no second-class Christians in God's Kingdom. If you are in Christ, you are white as snow (Isaiah 1:18). You are not a Christian with an asterisk after your name. You are cleaned, justified, and totally righteous. You are a full-fledged member of God's family.

> But where sin increased, **grace abounded all the more** (Romans 5:20).

Whatever thoughts run through your mind as you ponder your past, you must apply correct theology to your thinking. God loves you no less than He loves any other blood-bought sinner. There are no second-class Christians in God's Kingdom.

Remember, God does not love people because they have a short rap sheet. He does not love us because we were not abused. God does not love us because we have a slightly less sketchy past. God loves you because He loves you. God loved you while you were sinning (Romans 5:8). God loved you before He sent His Son (John 3:16). God loved you while you were hating Him (1 John 4:10).

God does not love you based on your performance; He loves you based on Christ's performance. If you are in Christ, God's love for you is the exact same love that He has for His Son.

When God looks at you, He sees you, hidden in Christ, and loves you with the same love He has for His Son.

God's love for His Son is the most intense love in the universe. That is the same love that God has for you because you are in Christ.

You are not, and cannot be, less loved by God because of your past or your present performance. You cannot spend enough time getting that straight in your mind. Remember, God is for you; He is not against you.

If you suffer deep wounds that have caused you lingering anxiety, you will need to work hard to realign your thinking with these truths. But it can be done and you can know joy and freedom from the shackles of the chains of your past.

There is a distinct possibility that your past has caused you to be angry at God Himself. Let the knowledge of Judgment Day forever remove that wicked thought. God has spared you from Judgment Day and He will throttle your enemies on Judgment Day. Remember, God is for you.

As you consider that history is headed toward the day when God will rightly judge and punish each and every misdeed, how can you know that and think that God Himself has committed a misdeed? Let that fact disavow any angry thought you may be harboring against God.

> Shall not the Judge of all the earth deal **justly** (Genesis 18:25)?

God has never done you wrong. God has never caused or permitted anything to happen in your life that wasn't for your good and for His glory. Study Judgment Day and that truth will become a reality to you. And remember that accusing God is a horrific sin that Jesus had to pay for on the Cross.

You Have Wounded Profoundly

Perhaps you have committed atrocious sins and you are living with a guilt that just won't go away. May I also tell you that your thinking is wrong?

- Your sins are great. His grace is greater.
- Your dirt is dirty. His cleansing is greater.
- Your shame is profound. His love stoops.

If you are in Christ, you are in Christ. You are not partially in, or kind of in, or sort of in. You are in. You are forgiven totally. You are cleansed thoroughly. You are loved profoundly.

Consider this laundry list of sinners who were members of the Corinthian Church.

> Do you not know that the unrighteous will not inherit the kingdom of God? Do not be deceived; neither **fornicators**, nor **idolaters**, nor **adulterers**, nor **effeminate**, nor **homosexuals**, nor **thieves**, nor the **covetous**, nor **drunkards**, nor **revilers**, nor **swindlers**, will inherit the kingdom of God. Such **were** some of you; but you were **washed**, but you were **sanctified**, but you were **justified** in the name of the Lord Jesus Christ and in the Spirit of our God (1 Corinthians 6:9–11).

Perhaps that list did not identify each and every sin and perversion, but it is a long enough list to include all of our perversions, including you and your bag of filth. But did you notice the other list? If you are in Christ, you are: washed, sanctified, and justified. No exceptions. Not even for you.

The Apostle Paul admitted he was a blasphemer, persecutor, and violent aggressor (1 Timothy 1:13). Paul was actually complicit in the murder of Christians, and yet God saved him and put him into service so that you can know that you are not beyond forgiveness and even service to the King.

> It is a trustworthy statement, deserving full acceptance, that Christ Jesus came into the world to save sinners, among whom I am

> **foremost** of all. Yet for this reason I found mercy, so that in me as the foremost, Jesus Christ might demonstrate His perfect patience **as an example** for those who would believe in Him for eternal life (1 Timothy 1:15–16).

That is a trustworthy statement, deserving of full acceptance. Do you believe that? If not, you need to ask God to help you get that riveted tightly into your heart. That is how Paul was able to live an abundant life of service without guilt. Knowing that he was spared from Judgment Day caused Paul to break out into a doxology in the very next verse.

> Now to the King eternal, immortal, invisible, the only God, be honor and glory forever and ever. Amen (1 Timothy 1:17).

That is what will happen to you when you fully believe that you, a vile, wretched, hell-bound sinner have been forgiven by God; you will break out in praise.

God is passionate about saving sinners and changing rebels into redeemed saints so He can receive honor and glory for being a just and compassionate God. He wants to rescue the worst of the worst and turn them into grateful worshipers. God wants to save the most broken and devastated and make them whole. God wants to purchase in-debt criminals and make them rich.

That is what He has done for us and He promises that He will avenge you, His covenant partner. Your enemies are God's enemies. Your foes are God's foes and He will avenge you.

Unless . . .

There is only one way that your enemies can escape the fierce fury of God's wrath. If your gracious God performs the same saving work on them that He performed on you, then Jesus will have received the wrath that your enemies deserve.

If your enemy is plucked from Adam and placed in Christ, your Savior will have received the intense rage that your enemy should have received.

Either your enemy or your Savior will receive the due punishment that your enemy deserves for the sins committed against you. Knowing that God's perfect justice will be satisfied in hell or was satisfied at the Cross should radically and totally affect you. This knowledge should move you:

- From self-pity to praise
- From disgusted to delighted
- From hateful to loving
- From hell-bound to happy
- From wounded to worshiping
- From vengeful to grace-full
- From bitter to blessed
- From resentful to rejoicing

Let Judgment Day bring you peace. But let it do more than that, let it grow you in love for people and for your God.

The Lord, The Saints' Avenger

"Because of the oppression of the weak and the groaning of the needy, I will now arise," says the Lord. "I will protect them from those who malign them" Psalm 12:5.

Never are the ungodly committed to a mistake more suicidal and fatal than when they lay the hand of injustice and oppression upon the saints of the Most High! God is for them. He is the Avenger of all those who put their trust in Him — the widow and the fatherless — and those who touch them touch the apple of His eye.

The God of the Christians is a *strong* Lord. All that strength is on the side of His people. "For the eyes of the Lord run to and fro throughout the whole earth, to show Himself STRONG in the behalf of those whose heart is perfect toward Him." Consider, O my soul, this truth, that the Lord is the strength of His people and the Avenger of all who are oppressed.

The Lord stands up for His oppressed ones. He is the Avenger of all such. *"It is God who avenges me,"* says David. Leave Him, O my soul, to vindicate your character, to redress your wrong, to rid you of your adversary, and He will bring forth your righteousness as the light, and your judgment as the noon-day. "O Lord, You have pleaded the causes of my soul."[1]

1. Excerpts from http://www.gracegems.org/Winslows/w03.htm.

Chapter 13

Anxiety Reliever #9: You Have a Father Who Lovingly Disciplines You

God does not turn scars into stars. God actually wounds you so He can heal you and grow you. And that, believe it or not, is anxiety reliever number nine.

> I am the true vine, and My Father is the **vinedresser**. Every branch in Me that does not bear fruit, He takes away; and every branch that bears fruit, **He prunes it** so that it may **bear more fruit** (John 15:1–2).

Jesus' words fly in the face of those who claim, "God will turn your scars into stars." That is the very opposite of what Jesus told His anxious disciples, and while this truth may be difficult to swallow initially, it is one of the most glorious truths in the Bible, that will forever change how you respond to difficult events.

In John 14–16, Jesus was preparing His disciples for future woes that might cause them to throw a pity party. Jesus told them that they would experience hard things, but those events were not to be considered bad luck. Hard things are for their good from the loving hand of their Father, the master gardener.

Nothing that happens to the Christian is arbitrary. Your life is not haphazard. The events of your life are not random. You are a branch and Jesus is the vine, and God is the divine gardener who does whatever is necessary to maximize your growth.

Without getting carried away with Jesus' gardening analogy, consider a rose bush in a garden.

- Most of the time, the gardener simply waters the rose.
- Occasionally the gardener fertilizes the plant.
- When necessary, the gardener will deadhead buds.
- The wise gardener will even cut back the entire bush once or twice a year, causing it to re-blossom and bear even more roses.

If our gardener were being observed by the uninitiated, they would likely overlook his typical tender care and conclude the gardener must be angry at the rose two or three times a year because he cuts off some roses that appear to have some life in them. What a mean gardener. Unfortunately, you and I are inclined to think about God the same way. We forget His constant provision and tend to see His pruning hand as either anger or indifference. It is not.

You can grieve God (Ephesians 4:30). You can hinder your relationship with God (1 Thessalonians 5:19). But you cannot do anything to cause God to dislike you or do mean things to you in retaliation for your behavior. Because you are in Christ, God loves you at all times as much as He loves His Son. Because you are in Christ:

- God loves you as much when you are sinning as when you are not sinning.
- God loves you the same when you use your mouth to worship Him or gossip.
- God loves you equally when you are serving the homeless or complaining about your home.

You cannot cause God to love you less because of your behavior. That is a dangerous truth, but it is truth nonetheless. And that truth must be remembered when the waves of adversity start to buffet your life. If you forget that God's love for you is the same as the love He has for His Son, you might think that God is a mean gardener. He is not.

God is a master gardener who will deadhead you, cut you back, or even cover you up to help you grow later. God is a wise, heavenly gardener who is willing to do painful things to help you bloom.

How does God want you to bloom? He wants you to sprout more love, joy, peace, patience, kindness, goodness, faithfulness, gentleness, and self-control (Galatians 5:22–23). Those fruits are so precious that God will do whatever it takes to grow those attributes in you, even if it hurts. That is clearly what Jesus was teaching the disciples, and us.

> My Father is glorified by this, that **you bear much fruit**, and so prove to be My disciples (John 15:8).

When God lovingly prunes His children, they bear much fruit; God is glorified and you are given assurance that you are in the vine, Jesus Christ. You can know you belong to the Master Gardener by inspecting the fruit in your life. When you see fruit, you can know you are His (2 Peter 1:8–11). God wants you to have assurance and He will prune you to give it to you as you bear fruit.

Turning a fist-shaking rebel into a saint brings great glory to God. Progressively restoring a busted sinner to their original design is the work that only He can do. And He will do whatever it takes to get you there.

WHY PAIN?

Why does God have to cause or permit painful things in order to sanctify us? First of all, we need it. Our fallen brains can be rather pigheaded. We get an idea and we tend to hold onto it so tenaciously that nothing but pain or suffering can drive it from our minds.

Second of all, pain works. Pain actually accomplishes the purpose God intended. Because we are both spiritual and physical beings, there is a connection between mind and body. There are times when only physical pain can teach us what we need to learn. Pain can affect us in positive ways.

The connection between the body and soul is inexplicable but undeniable. Sometimes pain can get our attention, teach us a lesson, and change our thinking and attitude.

You have seen the positive results of pain if you have ever lovingly and biblically spanked your child. What happens to the little monster who is pitching a fit and then feels the rod of correction? There is a sweetening in the child. Somehow, physical pain or discomfort speaks to our souls.

Our loving Father is willing to permit or cause pain to bring about a peaceable fruit of righteousness.

> God deals with you as with sons; for what son is there whom his father does not **discipline**? But if you are without discipline, of which

> all have become partakers, then you are illegitimate children and not sons. Furthermore, we had earthly fathers to discipline us, and we **respected** them; shall we not much rather be subject to the Father of spirits, and live? For they disciplined us for a short time as seemed best to them, but He disciplines us **for our good**, so that we may **share His holiness**. All discipline for the moment seems not to be joyful, but sorrowful; yet to those who have been trained by it, afterwards it yields the **peaceful fruit of righteousness** (Hebrews 12:7–11).

Out of love, your Heavenly Father inflicts or permits pain to grow you in holiness. Is it fun to go through it? No. Discipline is not fun, but it is effective and needed. Just look at all of the fruit that tribulation can bring:

> We also exult in **our tribulations**, knowing that tribulation brings about **perseverance**; and perseverance, proven **character**; and proven character, **hope**; and hope does not disappoint, because the love of God has been poured out within our hearts through the Holy Spirit who was given to us (Romans 5:3–5).

You may not be at the place where you exult in your tribulations, but you should be. Don't panic, you can get there because God wants you there and God is very good at getting what He wants. As you grow in your faith, you will increasingly exult in your tribulations.

How do you know how far along you are in the process? There are few faith markers that are more revealing than our response to difficulties. Take a moment to search through your memory banks. How did you respond when:

- You got fired
- Your child was naughty
- Your doctor gave you a bad report
- Another driver cut in front of you
- Someone dinged your car in the parking lot
- Your friend said cruel things about you behind your back

How you respond to challenges and annoyances is a telltale sign of the maturity of your faith. God wants you to respond the way Jesus responded to difficulties; by not sinning. If you are not at that level, then your kind God will prune you to grow you.

Your Idols

There is something else your loving Heavenly Father might be doing as He sanctifies you through discipline. God might be smashing the idols of your heart. After all, John Calvin rightly stated that our hearts are idol factories, and God graciously and jealously tears down those idols.

We don't typically build statues of our idols; we create mental idols that receive the affection, effort, and attention that belongs to God alone. Our idols take all sorts of shapes and sizes.

- Fame
- Spouse
- Property
- Knowledge
- Fashion
- Automobiles
- Jewelry
- Athletics
- Music
- Fortune
- Children
- Reputation
- Beauty
- Fitness
- Homes
- Education
- Success

Our heart idols can be virtually anything that we love, crave, and labor for in an ungodly way. God is a jealous God and He wants (and deserves) our affection, and He will do what it takes to turn your heart toward Him. This is an act of incredible kindness, as there is nothing better to delight in than God Himself.

We turn our fallen eyes on that which does not satisfy, grow, or fix us, but God sets His sights much higher for us. God wants us to worship and enjoy the best thing there is: Himself. What better thing could He point us toward? Nothing.

- God loves you too much to let you hold onto idols.
- God loves you too much to let you love the temporal trifles of this world.
- God loves you too much to let you worship the creation instead of the Creator.

Everything that God does for you is motivated by His great love. If you fail to remember that, you will quickly conclude that hardship is purposeless and even cruel. You will also conclude that God is distant, disengaged, or mad at you. When you remember that God loves you and desires your sanctification, then you will be able to exult in your tribulations.

This is not to suggest that God sends evil your way. God never does anything evil, but He does permit terrible things to happen, even to His children. God cannot sin and He will not sin against you, but God permits sin and He uses that sin, sinlessly.

We will explore that more in the next chapter, but for now, remember this rule: God does not send sinful calamities, but He does permit them. God Himself sends every other calamity that is not sinful (death, disease, bad weather, catastrophes). We see this very clearly in the Book of Job.

JOB

When we think of Job, we tend to imagine that Satan stumbled into Job and decided to mess with him. That is not the way the Bible describes it. Job 1:8 tells us that Satan was appearing before God's throne and God actually recommended that Satan buffet Job (Job 1:8). Satan then went about the business of destroying Job's property and and killing his children. Job initially responded like a stellar theologian:

> He said, "Naked I came from my mother's womb, and naked I shall return there. The **LORD gave** and the **LORD has taken** away. **Blessed** be the name of the LORD" (Job 1:21).

Job recognized God's sovereignty and that everything he possessed was actually on loan from God. Job understood what we tend to forget: that we own nothing and God owns everything.

God owns the earth, stars, air, water, hills, valleys, nations, rulers, celebrities, money, gold, silver, jewels, dirt, sand, flowers, trees, bugs, animals, and every single human being. Abraham Kuyper famously said, "There is not a square inch in the whole domain of our human existence over which Christ, who is Sovereign over all, does not cry, Mine!"[1]

Everything happens because God either causes it or permits it. God does not receive a text informing Him of your calamity; God either caused or permitted your calamity (Lamentations 3:38). When calamity comes calling, remember that it is God who dispatched her. Know that He sent calamity for your good.

---

1. https://www.goodreads.com/author/quotes/385896.Abraham_Kuyper.

- If your fingers are wrapped tightly around something that belongs to God, He will do whatever is necessary to loosen your grip.
- If you are idolizing anything more than God, He will pry it from you if necessary.
- If you brag, "Mine," God will reply with a "We'll see about that."

Have you ever experienced that? Have you ever lost something you loved? Could it be that God was actually being kind to you by removing your idol? Could your temporary loss possibly be a long-term gain because it has grown you in ways that no other means could have? Has your loss grown you in your love and dependence on God? Then it served its purpose well.

If you have been going through life responding to hard things by cursing God, growing bitter, moping, or going into a funk, then you are sinning (Job 1:22, 2:10), and you are missing out on the fruit that God wants to grow in you. In other words, you have been wasting your suffering. It is time to change that.

Well intentioned but sloppy theologians try to comfort sufferers by claiming, "God must be planning something big for you." That is wrong. God doesn't discover you are suffering and then give you a make-good. God does not find out about your lemons and turn them into lemonade. Your lemons are His gift to you to grow you in holiness.

Let's compare two different approaches and see which position is more helpful and hopeful. We will call the one view: Lemonade View (God turns your lemons into lemonade). We will compare that to the other view: Sanctification View (God disciplines you to grow you).

Tasmanian Devil

Your son is a terror. This little beast is driving you up the walls and causing you boatloads of anxiety.

The Lemonade View teaches that God will discover your frustration and perhaps provide some form of respite care for you.

The Sanctification View claims that God gave you a monster to grow you in patience, kindness, and reliance on Him. He is also using your little 666 to drive you to your knees and pray with the reliance and intensity that God deserves.

> Abide in Me, and I in you. As the branch cannot bear fruit of itself unless it **abides in the vine**, so neither can you unless you abide in Me (John 15:4).

God has knit together your little nightmare not to punish you, but to grow you. He wants you to abide in Him through His Word. God wants to use your precious little terror to humble you and make you look more like Jesus.

Bad Neighbors

Got annoying neighbors? They don't keep their property up, their kids are out of control and their dog uses your front lawn as his private potty.

The Lemonade View says that God will give you good neighbors once those piggy people move.

The Sanctification View teaches that God personally selected your nasty neighbors because you needed to learn some things. Perhaps you need to learn how to love neighbors who don't have your standards. Perhaps you need to learn that you have been loving your house too much. Perhaps you need to learn patience.

Your neighbors are not there by accident; they are there by God's design. He had you in mind when he moved "those people" next to you; it is your job to figure out why and grow.

Unbelieving Spouse

It is hard to know which is a harder family configuration: single parenthood or being unequally yoked. Living with someone who is not saved is downright hard.

The Lemonade View tries to comfort the saved spouse by saying, "God will make this better. I don't know how, but hang in there until He does."

The Sanctification View says that God determined that you would be married to that person long before He created the world. God chose your spouse because He knew that person was perfect for you. He knew that person would cause you to grow in ways that nothing else could. God knew that heathen you go to bed with would make you more loving, forgiving, and sacrificially generous. In other words, God knew your unsaved spouse would make you love others the way Jesus loves you.

Disease and Death

The doctor called and refused to give you the diagnosis. When you went to his office he informed you that you were sick. Very sick.

The Lemonade View says, "God was just as surprised as you and He did not want this to happen. Maybe God will heal you."

The Sanctification View reminds you that Lamentations 3:37–39 applies to you.

> Who is there who speaks and it comes to pass,
> Unless the **Lord has commanded it**?
> Is it not from the mouth of the Most High
> That **both good and ill** go forth?
> Why should any living mortal, or any man,
> Offer complaint in view of their sins?

The Sanctification View also reminds you that Romans 8 also applies to you.

> And we know that **God causes all things** to work together **for good** to those who love God, to those who are called according to **His purpose**. For those whom He foreknew, He also predestined to **become conformed to the image of His Son**, so that He would be the firstborn among many brethren; and these whom He **predestined**, He also called; and these whom He **called**, He also **justified**; and these whom He justified, He also **glorified** (Romans 8:28–30).

The Sanctification View causes us to conclude that God can do whatever He wants with His creation, including us. But we also know that everything He does for His children is for our good and His glory. Therefore, I know that my disease is good for me and if He chooses to end my life, then the One who predestined, called, and justified me, will also glorify me.

Not only does the Sanctification View give comfort and purpose to our suffering, but it should also bring joy, not depression. That's what Jesus said.

> These things I have spoken to you so that **My joy** may be in you, and that **your joy** may be made full (John 15:11).

Dear Christian, you will have troubles (John 16:33). Don't waste your troubles. Change your theology from the Lemonade to the Sanctification View, and your joy will be made full.

It Is Their Father's Hand That Chastens Them!

J.C. Ryle

Therefore it is that God's people pass through great tribulations; therefore it is they are often called upon to suffer the sting of affliction and anxiety — or weep over the grave of those whom they have loved as their own soul.

It is their Father's hand that chastens them! It is thus He weans their affection from things below, and fixes them on Himself. It is thus He trains them for eternity, and cuts the threads that bind their truant hearts to earth one by one.

No doubt such chastening is grievous for the time, but still it brings many a *hidden* grace to light. . . . We shall see those who have suffered most, shining among the brightest stars in the assembly of Heaven. "Our light affliction endures but for a moment, and it works for us a far more exceeding and eternal weight of glory!" 2 Corinthians 4:17.

The *purest gold* is that which has been longest in the refiner's furnace.

The *brightest diamond* is often that which has required the most grinding and polishing.

The saints are men who have come out of great tribulation — they are never left to perish in it.[2]

2. Excerpts from http://www.gracegems.org/2015/09/hand.html.

Chapter 14

Anxiety Reliever #10: You Have a Pre-arranged Plan

The world says you can do anything if you put your mind to it and believe in yourself. Jesus disagrees. That is why anxiety reliever number 10 infuriates the self-esteem movement.

> I am the vine, you are the branches; he who abides in Me and I in him, he bears much fruit, for apart from Me **you can do nothing** (John 15:5).

According to the One who holds the world together by the word of His power (Hebrews 1:3), you and I can do absolutely, positively nothing without Him. The Greek word for nothing means: nothing.

> For **in Him** we live and move and exist (Acts 17:28).

This is the doctrine of sovereignty. If God is not nice, this doctrine would be a nightmare. But God is love, and that makes the doctrine of sovereignty one of God's most comforting attributes.

You and I can't do anything without God willing it. He is far greater and we are far more pathetic than we can imagine.

- Can you make your hair grow?
- Can you cause yourself to grow taller?
- Can you create more or less digestive juice in your stomach?

We can't cause our blood to flow faster, our nails to grow longer or our skin to stop sagging. We control nothing about ourselves and we can certainly control nothing outside of ourselves. God is the One who controls all things. God is not merely in charge of the big things; He is in control of each and every molecule in the universe. Naturalistic explanations cannot account for the energy, wisdom and design of the cosmos, but the Bible does.

> **In his hand** is the life of every creature and the breath of all mankind (Job 12:10; NIV).

God is omniscient; He knows every detail of every event, activity, thought, dream, everything. Here are just three of dozens of verses that describe God's omniscience.

> But the very hairs of your head are all numbered (Matthew 10:30).

> He counts the number of the stars; He gives names to all of them (Psalm 147:4).

> O Lord, You have searched me and known me. You know when I sit down and when I rise up; You understand my thought from afar (Psalm 139:1–2).

The doctrine of sovereignty rejoices that God knows the end from the beginning (Isaiah 46:10). He not only knows what is going to happen, He has ordained every event for all time. Undoubtedly you are starting to ask questions like, is God responsible for evil?

God never sins, nor does He cause anyone to sin. Remember, God permits sin and He uses sin, sinlessly. God does not author sin, but He uses it when people commit it. God does not get credit for sin, but He gets credit for using it for our good. The Westminster Confession of Faith, chapter 3, states:

> God from all eternity, did, by the most wise and holy counsel of His own will, freely, and unchangeably **ordain whatsoever** comes to pass; yet so, as thereby neither is God the author of sin, nor is violence offered to the will of the creatures; nor is the liberty or contingency of second causes taken away, but rather established (emphasis added).[1]

1. http://www.reformed.org/documents/wcf_with_proofs/index.html?body=/documents/wcf_with_proofs/ch_III.html.

Defining Terms

Sovereignty: God independently rules over all things and determines every detail of every event by willing or permitting each and every activity under the sun. God is not sovereign in principle only, He is sovereign in practice and His will is never thwarted. God works all things by the counsel of His will (Ephesians 1:11).

Providence: Literally "seeing beforehand," God not only sees ahead, but determines and guides all things to their predetermined end as ordained by our sovereign God.

Benevolence: God is all good and desires to do good things for His creatures.

Concurrence: God works with sinful human beings to accomplish His prearranged plan. Therefore, God gets credit for everything that is good and we get credit for everything that is bad.

Theodicy: Defending God's sovereignty and kindness in light of evil in the world. It seeks to answer the question, "Why does a good God allow evil in the world?"

When we learn the answer to that question, we will never need to be anxious about difficult events ever again. So let's take a closer look at painful subjects like evil and calamity.

2-2-2 Principle

There are only two types of people in this world: the saved and the unsaved. There are no other biblical distinctions offered to define people; a person is either a child of God or a child of the devil.

God orchestrates all events though two means: He either causes or permits each and every event. God causes all non-sinful events and He permits all sinful actions.

God is doing two things for each of these two groups of people. God is either pouring out His wrath on sinners (Romans 1:18), or He is using tragedy to call them to repentance (Luke 13:1–5). God is either disciplining His children (Hebrews 12:4–11), or He is preparing them to minister to others in the future (2 Corinthians 1:3–4).

That means God causes or permits evil to descend on your life in order to do something good for you. No calamity that has ever befallen you is purposeless. It is for your good and for His glory (Romans 8:28).

God is not 911 when something horrible happens. God doesn't discover you are experiencing a hardship and then try to figure out a way to rescue you. If you are going through something difficult, your loving Father has either caused it or permitted it. But make no mistake about it, He is trying to do something FOR you in it. Remember, God is FOR you, He is not against you.

Comfort

The doctrine of sovereignty should cause us to receive each and every event in our lives with Romans 8:28 in view and conclude, "It is well with my soul." If God does everything that is best for us, then we can receive the hard things in life recognizing that they are actually good for us.

God loves you too much to let you live comfortably in complacency. God loves you too much to not wound you in an effort to heal and grow you. God loves you too much to let you hold onto idols. God loves you too much to not do hard things for you so that you can enjoy being conformed into the image of Jesus Christ.

Difficulty in life could also be sent by God to prepare you for something in the future. He could be preparing you for ministry, service, or a new assignment. Perhaps He is humbling you so you don't get puffed up when He gives you a promotion. The possibilities are endless.

Whether the tragedy is sinful (theft, murder, violence, bullying), or not sinful (bad weather, disease, bankruptcy, destruction), we must remember that nothing happens outside of God's will. It is your job, and your job alone, to figure out what God is trying to do FOR you. How do you do that?

1. Pray and ask God for wisdom (more on this in the next chapter).
2. Examine your walk. Are there sins that need to be mortified? Is there a lack of a particular fruit in your life?
3. Study your Bible on the subject you are experiencing.
4. Receive godly council.

You may not figure it out immediately, but it is almost certain you will figure it out in the future. How many times have you heard a Christian say something like this: "When I lost my job, I thought it was the worst thing in the world. But I prayed hard and felt God's comfort through His Word more than at any other time in my life." There are some things that we may not figure out until we get to heaven, but most times, we will be able to figure out what God is doing for us.

Let's work through some very common calamities so you can be prepared when your calamity inevitably strikes.

Weather Tragedies

God is not the Red Cross who cleans up messes after Mother Nature wreaks havoc. God is in control of the weather.

> For to the snow **He says**, "Fall on the earth,"
> And to the downpour and the rain, "Be strong."
> He seals the hand of every man,
> That all men may know **His work**.
> Then the beast goes into its lair
> And remains in its den.
> Out of the south comes the storm,
> And out of the north the cold.
> From the breath of God ice is made,
> And the expanse of the waters is frozen.
> Also with moisture **He loads** the thick cloud;
> **He disperses** the cloud of His lightning.
> It changes direction, turning around by **His guidance**,
> That it may do whatever **He commands** it
> On the face of the inhabited earth.
> Whether for correction, or for His world,
> Or for loving kindness, He **causes it** to happen (Job 37:6–13).

Did your basement get flooded in the storm? You can thank God; He sent the rain. Do not think you were simply swept up in the flood. God sends a storm with everyone in mind who is caught in the torrent. God doesn't blanket a region in rain because He wants to destroy Larry's basement, but your loss is unfortunate collateral damage. If your basement got flooded, it is because God wanted it wet.

If someone put a hose in your basement window, He did not cause that but He did permit that sinful event because He must have wanted the basement He is loaning you to get six inches of water. It is not a sin for God to destroy the house that He is loaning you.

It is now your job to figure out why God wants you to deal with this calamity. What is He trying to teach you? Is there a sin in your life that needs to be mortified that only half a foot of water could kill? Is your home your idol? Is He draining your savings because you were going to spend it on something sinful?

UNEMPLOYMENT

If you do not have a job at the moment, it is because God wants you unemployed. That may strike you hard initially, but consider the option: God is sovereign, except when it comes to getting you a job.

When we try to defend God's character by saying God doesn't want us to be unemployed, we are merely kicking the theological can down the street. If God knew you were going to get fired and He didn't stop it, then He is not omnipotent or He is kind of cruel. To suggest that God was unaware of your job loss compromises His omniscience and omnipotence.

> Who can command things to happen without the Lord's permission? Does not the Most High send both **calamity** and **good**? Then why should we, mere humans, complain when we are punished for our sins (Lamentations 3:37–39; NLT)?

What might God want to do FOR you as you sit at home unemployed? The options are many.

- He wants you to pray more.
- He wants you to rely on Him more.
- He wants you to read your Bible more.
- He wants you to trust His promises more.
- He wants to pry an idol from your hands.
- He wants you to spend time examining your walk.
- He wants you to heal some relationships with your family.
- He wants you to wait until He prepares the next job He wants you to have.

The following paragraph was posted on our Facebook page by a fellow named Ralph Schaefer in the comment section of a video we produced titled, "God Does Not Turn Your Lemons into Lemonade."[2]

2. https://www.youtube.com/watch?v=1N722YWUoy4.

> I was out of work for two years and it was one of the **best things** that ever happened to my family. All of us grew closer to the Lord and to each other while we waited for the job He was preparing for me.

That is what the Lord did for Ralph. What is He trying to do for you? Your friends, family, and spouse cannot tell you what God is trying to do for you; it is your job alone to figure it out. The doctrine of sovereignty should comfort you as you do.

Sickness

It is not a sin for God to give you an illness. If you are sick, it is because God has made you ill. He may have used secondary natural causes, but God is the author of health and illness.

> See now that I, I am He, and there is no god besides Me; it is I who put to death and give life. **I have wounded** and it is **I who heal**, and there is no one who can deliver from My hand (Deuteronomy 32:39).

Again, if you claim your illness is caused by someone or something other than God, you still end up with the same question: "Why didn't God stop this from happening?" Or you will be forced to ask, "Why doesn't God heal me NOW?" It is more biblically sound and far more comforting to know that our Heavenly Physician is the One who makes sick and He is the One who makes well.

> Bless the Lord, O my soul, and forget none of His benefits; who pardons all your iniquities, who **heals all your diseases**; who redeems your life from the pit, who crowns you with lovingkindness and compassion (Psalm 103:2–4).

This is radical, but when you and I understand that God heals us and makes us sick, we can praise Him for both. Does that mean we say "Yippee skippee" while we are lurched over a bucket? No, but we can know that the God who loves us does not have anything befall us that is not for our good.

There are three more reasons God might cause you to be sick:

1. Lord's Supper: if you fail to examine yourself rightly prior to taking the Lord's Supper, in His mercy, God might make you ill to move you toward examining yourself for ongoing, unrepentant, unconfessed sin in your life.

> Therefore whoever eats the bread or drinks the cup of the Lord in an **unworthy manner**, shall be guilty of the body and the blood of the Lord. But a man must examine himself, and in so doing he is to eat of the bread and drink of the cup. For he who eats and drinks, eats and **drinks judgment** to himself if he does not judge the body rightly. For this reason many among you are **weak** and **sick**, and a **number sleep** (1 Corinthians 11:27–30).

2. God might make you sick to demonstrate His healing power. He did this in John 9 with a man who had been blind since birth. Jesus told the disciples that the man was born blind so that the works of God might be displayed in him (John 9:3). It is possible He is doing that with you too.
3. Perhaps God is using your illness to witness to others (2 Corinthians 12:9). It is possible that God has made you ill to model how a Christian wrestles with illness and even dies well. Perhaps your children need to see their Mom or Dad die with Christian confidence so they too will be confident.

God does not play catch-up. God does not have a backlog of emails He hasn't read yet. God is not a first responder; He is the first causer. Sinful events are the responsibility of man, non-sinful difficulties are directly from the hand of God: both fall under His providential will. This goes for every circumstance in your life:

- If you get into a car accident, God wanted your car to have a ding.
- If you lose your wallet, God took it from you.
- If you stub your toe, God wanted your little piggy to be in pain.

God regularly uses secondary means to accomplish His will for your life. If someone rammed into your car in a fit of anger, or if someone sinfully stole your wallet or wacked your tootsie with a hammer, God did not commit those sins against you. But God permitted it because He ordained it to happen. God does not sin when He wounds you; He is doing something for you.

Does God like it when you are hurt? Of course not; but He is willing to wound or even allow you to be sinned against if that is what is needed for your good and His glory (Romans 8:28). A loving earthly father doesn't rejoice when he lovingly spanks his beloved child. Our loving Heavenly Father doesn't rejoice either.

Make no mistake, it is right and human to weep when bad things happen (Ecclesiastes 3:4), but we have hope and joy knowing that God isn't just in our messes; He causes them for our ultimate good. Nothing happens to you that is not a part of God's benevolent plan for you.

Death

It is a sin to murder (Deuteronomy 5:17). It is not a sin for God to take your life (Job 1:21). If it is a sin for God to take life, then He sinned when He killed Uzzah (2 Samuel 6:7) and Ananias and Sapphira (Acts 5:1–11), and a gazillion pagans in the Old Testament.

God is the author of life (1 Timothy 6:13), sustainer of life (Acts 17:25, 28) and God is the One who ends our lives (Psalm 139:16). Murder is a sin, but if God takes a human life it is not a sin. If God is the One who sustains your life, and He is, then God is responsible for when your life is no longer sustained. God can send illness directly or He can use secondary causes. If you are sick, it may have happened due to exposure to asbestos or tainted food, but God is still the One who decides whether you are going to live another day or not.

This theology has always been understood by Christians. Consider this statement from the 1689 London Baptist Confession of Faith, chapter 3:

> God hath **decreed in Himself**, from all eternity, by the most wise and holy counsel of His own will, freely and unchangeably, **all things, whatsoever** comes to pass; yet so as thereby is God neither the author of sin nor hath fellowship with any therein; nor is violence offered to the will of the creature, nor yet is the liberty or contingency of second causes taken away, but rather established; in which appears His wisdom in disposing **all things**, and power and faithfulness in accomplishing His decree. (Isaiah 46:10; Ephesians 1:3–5, 11; Hebrews 6:17; Romans 9:15, 18; James 1:13; 1 John1:5; Acts 4:27–28; John 19:11; Numbers 23:19) (emphasis added).[3]

If God were wicked, then you might complain about your illness or death date. But God is good and He scheduled your death before eternity began

3. http://www.1689.com/confession.html#Ch. 3.

(Psalm 139:16). If God has decided today is the day that you will die, you will die. If God has determined that you, like Hezekiah, are going to live another 15 years, then nothing can end your life for the next decade and a half (2 Kings 20:6).

Think about how comforting that truth is. Why should we worry about death when the most gracious being in the universe has determined the absolute best date for us to die? That date is not only best for us, but for our spouses, our children, our business, our church, our everything. Why on earth would we think WE know the best day we should die?

Perhaps you have a fear of flying. You shouldn't. God has determined your birth date and your death date and there is nothing you can do to change that. If you don't fly because you have a paralyzing fear, you should know that God could kill you on the ground as easily as He could kill you in the air.

Should we be reckless with our lives? Of course not; we do not tempt God or practice unwise stewardship. But flying and driving are hardly reckless activities.

There is an old joke that goes, "I am not afraid of flying because I think it is my day to die, but what if it is the day to die for one of the other passengers?" OK, what if it is?

When a plane crashes and everyone perishes, it is because God wanted each and every one of those people to die that day. Nobody dies randomly.

Perhaps you have heard of a crash survivor who lives a tormented life because they survived and others didn't. Perhaps you have heard of people who live with a cloud over their head because they missed the flight that crashed and killed everyone on board. If they understood the doctrine of sovereignty they would not wonder. They would simply conclude, "God wanted me to live."

Think of Joseph. This young man endured hardship after hardship:

- Mistreatment by rotten brothers
- Physical and verbal abuse
- His brothers wanted to murder him
- He was kidnapped
- He was separated from family, friends, and all things familiar
- He was sold into slavery
- Powerful people slandered him
- He suffered false imprisonment

Joseph's blessed life in Israel was totally upended and replaced with a different life in Egypt. All of that was at the hands of his brothers. And to Whom did Joseph give credit when he was reunited with his rascally siblings?

> As for you, **you meant evil** against me, but **God meant it for good** in order to bring about this present result, to preserve many people alive (Genesis 50:20).

God permitted Joseph's brothers to sin against him so Joseph could rescue Israel from starvation. If all of the Jews had starved to death, then we would not have a Savior. God may not use you for something that profound, but you must know that He is using every calamity in your life for His glory.

If you still think that this teaching is radical, may I point you to the Cross? The single greatest tragedy of all time was God's prearranged plan.

> Peter said, "Men of Israel, listen to these words: Jesus the Nazarene, a man attested to you by God with miracles and wonders and signs which God performed through Him in your midst, just as you yourselves know — this Man, delivered over by the **predetermined plan** and **foreknowledge** of God, you nailed to a cross by the hands of godless men and put Him to death. But God raised Him up again, putting an end to the agony of death, since it was impossible for Him to be held in its power" (Acts 2:22–24).

God created the world, knowing that Adam would sin, so He could orchestrate four thousand years of human history so His Son could be born at just the right time so He would be crucified for sinners (Galatians 4:4–7).

God used sinful men (concurrence) to crush His only Son (Isaiah 53:10). The death of Jesus was not a tragedy; it was a triumph that was the culmination of God's prearranged plan. Jesus' death was not a disaster; it was a victory.

Your God has a pre-arranged plan for you too. He made you to save you and do the work that He has planned for you during the days He has built for you to inhabit (Psalm 139:16).

> For we are His workmanship, created in Christ Jesus **for good works**, which God **prepared beforehand** so that we would walk in them (Ephesians 2:10).

Your loving Lord has already determined the date when you are going to go to be with Him. Know that it is the absolute best possible timing. You might think it is too soon, but God does not. You might think it isn't the ideal time, but God does. You can trust Him to know better because He is sovereign and He loves you.

If this is new to you, please wrestle with all of these verses in this chapter and resolve this issue today. It is much easier to cope with tragedy, illness, and death when you have worked through the doctrine of sovereignty *before* it happens. God appoints both prosperity and poverty; He humbles and He exalts (1 Samuel 2:7). He makes us ill and He heals our diseases (Psalm 103:2–4). The Lord determines our birth date (Psalm 139) and our death date (Psalm 31:15). The Lord comforts (2 Corinthians 7:6) and the Lord brings crosses (Isaiah 45:7).

Know that God loves you. Know that God is sovereign over everything. Know that you can do nothing without Him and let that be your comfort when your King sends you a hard thing.

The Lord's Rod Has a Voice!

James Buchanan, 1840

The day of adversity teaches us the great lesson of **our entire and constant dependence on God**. But a little while before, we were rejoicing in the midst of prosperity — our health was sound, our business prosperous, our families entire. But the sudden stroke has come which has smitten . . .

our *bodies* with disease, our *business* with bankruptcy,
or our *families* with death.
And that stroke has come from the Lord's hand!
Oh! in such circumstances, we are impressively taught . . .
that we are absolutely in God's power;
that all that we have is at His sovereign disposal;
that we depend on Him, day by day, continually for . . .
our personal preservation, our worldly prosperity,
our domestic comfort,
for all, in short, that we desire or need on earth.[4]

4. Excerpts from http://www.gracegems.org/2015/10/rod.html.

Chapter 15

Anxiety Reliever #11: You Can Talk to God

When you are in trouble, who you gonna call?

- Ghostbusters
- Blondie
- 911
- James Taylor
- An attorney

While these all may or may not be good options, you have the ability to call someone who truly cares and who can help you in each and every precarious situation: your omnipotent God. And that is anxiety reliever number 11.

> Truly, truly, I say to you, if you **ask the Father** for anything in My name, He will give it to you. Until now you have asked for nothing in My name; ask and you will receive, so that **your joy may be made full** (John 16:23–24).

A prisoner who has just been arrested gets one call; you and I can call our omnipotent God anytime, day or night, as often as we want, and He will do what is best for us. It is amazing how much we like to talk to people about our problems but we forget that God, the One who can actually relieve us of our burdens, petitions us to pray to Him.

> Be **anxious for nothing**, but in everything, by **prayer** and supplication with thanksgiving let your **requests** be made known to God. And the **peace of God**, which surpasses all comprehension, will guard your hearts and your minds in Christ Jesus (Philippians 4:6–7).

Because we can talk to God about anything, we should be anxious about nothing. Prayer and anxiety go together like the Minnesota Vikings and Super Bowl champions. Like Hollywood and morality. Like the federal government and efficiency. Knowing that you can talk to the God who cares for you should eliminate your worries.

Never think your request is too small. Never feel like you are troubling God. He wants you, commands you, to cast all of your cares on Him and leave them there.

> . . . casting all your **anxiety** on Him, because He **cares** for you (1 Peter 5:7).

Don't cast your cares on God and then reel them back in so you can mull them over some more; cast your cares and leave them with the One who is able to handle them.

> And if we know He hears us in **whatever we ask**, we know that we have the requests which we have asked from Him (1 John 5:15).

God hears every single prayer and request you make, and He will give you the absolute best answer to your petition. Notice, that doesn't mean He is going to give you the answer you want. God answers all prayers with one of four options: yes, no, later, or something else. Know that He will always answer in the best way *for* you.

This is not to suggest we should live life recklessly and never plan for the future. We are to be good stewards of time and talents and plan wisely for the future, but we should not be burdened with concerns as we do. God cares for the birds of the air, but they still have to go find worms. He expects us to do the same. If you are on a boat that is sinking, ask God to rescue you, and then get busy looking for a lifeboat. Do you have a needy relative? Pray that God will provide and then start helping (1 Timothy 5:8). Pray that God will help your child pass chemistry, then help him study his periodic chart. Casting your cares on the Lord does not mean we can go the mall while our house is burning down.

PRAYERS AND SUPPLICATIONS

There is a difference between prayers and supplications. Prayers include thanks, confession, repentance, and praise. Supplications are requests. Too often our prayers are littered with supplications. If your children only spoke to you when they wanted something from you, that would indicate your child is ungrateful and sees you as only a bank or dispenser of stuff.

Furthermore, we are to bring our prayers and supplications with thanksgiving (Philippians 4:6). There are at least seven reasons for this.

1. There is always something to give thanks for. No matter how abysmal your circumstances are, if you can pray, you have something to be grateful for.
2. To only make requests without ever thanking God for the many blessings He has bestowed on you is rude and reveals a heart of ingratitude.
3. It borders on accusatory to only ask and never thank.
4. Giving thanks promotes joy in us.
5. Going through all of God's blessings reminds us that He truly does care about us.
6. Constant petitions without thanksgiving can result in resignation and murmuring.
7. It is presumptuous to never thank God.

Yes, we can make supplications, but to only ask and never thank is just bad manners.

- Ask God to protect your children, but thank Him for all of the years He already has.
- Ask God to help you with finances, but thank Him for all of the money He has given you over the years.
- Ask God to make your left knee pain to go away, but don't forget to thank Him for the lack of pain in your right knee.
- Ask God to help you get your car fixed after the accident, but don't forget to thank Him for all of the days you have driven safely.
- Ask God for a new job, but don't forget to thank Him for the healthy body you have that allows you to work.

Even if your life is a disaster of Job-like proportions, you can still thank Him for His attributes. You can always thank Him for Jesus, the Cross and salvation.

PRAYING PRECISELY

When God presents something to you that could cause you anxiety, remember that this is a faith issue and He is trying to grow you. Rotten things are not happening to you without purpose; there is design in your suffering/pain/disappointment. Knowing that should cause us to pray rightly.

There is nothing wrong with praying, "Lord, please help my child to behave better." But knowing that God wants to use your disobedient child to grow you, perhaps a better prayer might be, "Lord, You have given me the child that is best for me. Would You please help me learn exactly what You would have me learn from him? Please grow me in patience and kindness as I strive to be more like You. Would You please help me model You for my little terrorizer?"

Perhaps you are unequally yoked. There is nothing wrong with praying, "Lord, please save my spouse." But knowing that God has provided the perfect spouse for you, perhaps you should also pray, "Lord, would You please help me to submit to You and treat my unsaved spouse the way You treated me before You saved me? Would You please grow me in love, gentleness, and self-control so that my life undergirds my testimony?"

Pray for your situation, but be mindful that God is using your circumstances to conform you into the image of His Son; then pray accordingly. You will be praying "in the Spirit" (Ephesians 6:18), based on His Word, knowing that God is seeking to grow you.

Consider the difference in these requests to God.

- Lord, let my child do well on this test so I don't have to worry *vs.* help me to rely on you and not be anxious for my child.
- Lord, please take away my anxiety *vs.* teach me what I am supposed to learn during this challenging situation so I can grow to be more like Jesus.
- Lord, make this stop *vs.* show Your strength mightily in my weakness.

There are few inappropriate requests most Christians make, but very few Christians pray precisely for the right things.

PRAY PERSISTENTLY

If you perceive God is not answering your prayers immediately, don't fret. God will answer at the best time with the best answer. Perhaps He is withholding an answer to your prayer because He is teaching you to pray more regularly.

> Rejoice always; **pray without ceasing**; in everything give thanks; for this is God's will for you in Christ Jesus (1 Thessalonians 5:16–18).

Too many books have been written that demand you pray the way the author prays. While it is nice that his prayer method works for him, we can't make laws where there are no laws. Paul says we should pray persistently, but he doesn't tell us exactly when and for how long. Figure out what works for you and the Lord will grow you in the duration, intensity, focus, desire, and passion in your prayers.

Pray Personally

Remember that God is transcendent, but He is also your Father and He cares for you. That means we should talk to Him personally. That does not mean flippant or casual, but we should talk to God like we are talking to a person who loves us.

A few years ago, Rabbi Schmuley Boteach actually said to me, "You evangelicals pray to God as if you are actually talking to Him and He is listening to you." Duh. While I have no idea what Schmuley is thinking when he prays, Christians should talk to God as if He is listening, because He is.

It always perplexes me when Christians say, "I just feel like my prayers hit the ceiling and don't go any higher." That is wrong for several reasons.

- Our God is in the heavens, but He stoops to hear our prayers. He isn't sitting on His throne reading through a prayer stack, He bends an ear to hear you.
- It doesn't matter how we feel about our prayers. God says He hears them whether we feel like He does or not.
- This statement makes it sound like some of our prayers get above the ceiling because they are good prayers or we are really focusing, but others don't. God does not hear our prayers because of the way we pray them. God hears our prayers because of Jesus.

It is Jesus who makes our prayers perfect, not our concentration or eloquence. Think of it like the little boy who gathers flowers for his mother.

As he runs into the house to deliver them, his father stops him and says, "Son, I'll take them from here." As Dad walks to deliver the flowers to Mom, he plucks out the weeds and dandelions and replaces them with roses and lilies. Then he delivers the beautiful bouquet on behalf of the son. That is what Jesus does with our prayers.

PRAY WITH PRAISE

Praying and praising God at the same time relieves anxiety. Not only are the Psalms set to music, but we see two examples of godly men who praised God even while they faced a horrific circumstance.

The first man who prayed with praise is an Old Testament prophet named Habakkuk. The Book of Habakkuk opens with a prayer from the prophet to rescue the nation of Israel as it imploded from lawlessness and violence (Habakkuk 1:2–4).

God's response to Habakkuk's question is a lulu. He informs Habakkuk that He is going to do something astonishing and wonderful (Habakkuk 1:5). God was going to send the most wicked, vicious, sadistic nation ever, the Chaldeans, to take the nation of Israel into captivity (Habakkuk1: 5–10). Say what?

God's astonishing plan for the nation of Israel was to ordain an imminent attack from the most terrifying nation on the planet. God was going to do this for three reasons:

1. He was being faithful to His Mosaic covenant, which promised curses for disobedience.
2. He would be glorified by one day delivering the Jews from captivity in faithfulness to His Abrahamic covenant.
3. The Jews would learn their lesson and commit to being a set-apart nation from whence the Messiah would come.

What looked like a nightmare to Habakkuk was ultimately astonishing and wonderful. Remember that the next time you see storm clouds on your horizon: God only does what is best for us and for His glory. Your story won't be added to the Bible, but make no mistake, God is no less involved in your life than in the lives of every person in the Bible.

After God and Habakkuk shared several exchanges, Habakkuk offered up a final prayer to God with praise on stringed instruments.

Though the fig tree should not blossom
And there be no fruit on the vines,
Though the yield of the olive should fail
And the fields produce no food,
Though the flock should be cut off from the fold
And there be no cattle in the stalls,
Yet I will exult in the Lord,
I **will rejoice** in the God of my salvation.
The Lord God is my strength,
And He has made my feet like hinds' feet,
And makes me walk on my high places (Habakkuk 3:17–19).

Habakkuk played music to accompany his prayers and the result, despite the horrifying future he faced, was to praise God. The next time you find yourself being attacked by a ferocious nation, or your children, offer up prayers with praise and watch your mood rise.

Habakkuk was not the only man who sang when things looked bleak. Paul found himself in a jail in Philippi that would undoubtedly make San Quentin look like the Ritz. And what did he do while he sat in chains?

> But about midnight Paul and Silas were **praying and singing hymns of praise** to God, and the prisoners were listening to them (Acts 16:25).

Singing hymns of praise while praying brings joy because thanksgiving and joy are connected. When we think and sing about what God has done for us, that brings us joy. Do you need some joy? Start praying and praising God with thanksgiving.

> O come, let us **sing for joy** to the Lord, let us shout **joyfully** to the rock of our salvation. Let us come before His presence with **thanksgiving**, let us shout **joyfully** to Him with psalms (Psalm 95:1–2).

Need joy? Sing praise to the Lord and watch Him change your heart.

Pray the Word

God wants you to speak from your heart, but it is imperative that our hearts are instructed by God's Word. That is what Jesus meant when He said we should ask for anything in His name (John 16:23). When our prayers are in alignment with God's Word, then our requests are in alignment with what God is doing. When prayers are not in alignment with God's Word, then they are most likely sinful and God is not committed to respond.

Imagine your child approached you with a request. Which request would you be likely to answer positively?

> **Request #1:** Mom, Dad, would you please help me to be a more obedient child?
>
> **Request #2:** Mom, Dad, give me lots of toys for Christmas.

The more our prayers are aligned with God's desires, the more we are praying in alignment with His will and we are "working with Him" in the same direction toward the same goals.

There is a very helpful book that might aid you in that endeavor. Ken Boa wrote two prayer books based on praying the Scriptures (*Face to Face*).[1] Each prayer contains the following elements:

- Adoration
- Renewal
- Intercession
- Thanksgiving
- Confession
- Petition
- Affirmation

Each one of these categories contains multiple Bible verses to align your prayers with God's Word. Here is just one example from morning affirmations:

Submitting to God

I submit myself and my life to you, O God:

In view of your mercy, O God, may I present my body as a living sacrifice, holy and pleasing to You, which is my reasonable service. May I not be conformed to the pattern of this world but be transformed by the renewing of my mind, that I may prove your will is good and acceptable and perfect (Romans 12:1–2).

Adoration and Thanksgiving

For who You are and what You have done, accept my thanks, O Lord:

1. Ken Boa, *Face to Face: Praying the Scriptures for Intimate Worship* (Grand Rapids, MI: Zondervan Publishing House, 1997).

Blessed are You, O Lord,
For You have heard the voice of my prayers.
You are my strength and my shield;
My heart trusts in You, and I am helped. My heart greatly rejoices,
And I will give thanks to You in song (Psalm 28:6-7).

Examination

Holy Spirit, search my heart and reveal to me any unconfessed sin You find in me:

Search me, O God, and know my heart;
Test me and know my anxious thoughts.
See if there is any offensive way in me,
And lead me in the way everlasting (Psalm 139:23-24).

Lord, I thank You for the forgiveness You promised when You said:

"Come now, let us reason together:
Though your sins are like scarlet, they shall be as white as snow;
Though they are red as crimson,
They shall be like wool" (Isaiah 1:18).

My Identity in Christ

I rejoice, Lord Jesus, in the identity I have in You:

I have been crucified with You, and it is no longer I who live, but You who live in me; and the life which I now live in the flesh, I live by faith in You, the Son of God, who loved me, and delivered Yourself up for me (Galatians 2:20).

I have forgiveness from the penalty of sin because You died for me:

But You, O God, demonstrate Your own love for us in that, while we were still sinners, Christ died for us (Romans 5:8).

It goes on and on, but you get the point. Now imagine praying like that as you praise and petition God for your children, your career, your belongings, your church, the world, your neighbors, your leaders.

There is another book that you might find helpful, *The Valley of Vision*. Be warned, this Puritan prayer book is not for the meek at heart, but your heart and mind will be changed with these thoroughly biblical prayers. Here is just one prayer, titled "Morning Needs."

> O God the author of all good, I come to Thee for the grace another day will require for its duties and events. I step out into a wicked world; I carry about with me an evil heart. I know that without Thee I can do nothing, that everything with which I shall be concerned, however harmless in itself, may prove an occasion of sin or folly, unless I am kept by Thy power. Hold Thou me up and I shall be safe.
>
> Preserve my understanding from subtlety of error, my affections from love of idols, my character from stain of vice, my profession from every form of evil. May I engage in nothing in which I cannot implore Thy blessing, and in which I cannot invite Thy inspection. Prosper me in all lawful undertakings, or prepare me for disappointments. Give me neither poverty nor riches. Feed me with food convenient for me, lest I be full and deny Thee and say, Who is the Lord? or be poor, and steal, and take Thy name in vain.
>
> Teach me how to use the world and not abuse it, to improve my talents, to redeem my time, to walk in wisdom toward those without, and in kindness to those within, to do good to all men, and especially to my fellow Christians. And to Thee be the glory.[2]

You will find dozens of prayers like that in *The Valley of Vision*. These prayers will focus your brain, stir your heart, and ensure you pray in alignment with the Word.

More Confidence, Less Complaining

We all feel a need to talk to a sympathetic ear when times are tough. That alone should drive us to our knees to talk to the single most sympathetic One in the universe: the Lord Jesus Christ.

> Therefore, since we have a great high priest who has passed through the heavens, Jesus the Son of God, let us hold fast our confession. For we do not have a high priest who cannot **sympathize** with our weaknesses, but One who has been tempted in all things as we are, yet without sin. Therefore let us draw near **with confidence** to the throne of grace, so that we may receive mercy and **find grace to help in time of need** (Hebrews 4:14–16).

2. Arthur Bennett, *The Valley of Vision* (Edinburgh, UK: Banner of Truth, 1975).

Why would we want to talk to anyone else when we can talk to Him? Just consider all of the things you can talk to Him about and how that will affect you.

> In prayer all things here below vanish, and nothing seems important but holiness of heart and the salvation of others. In prayer all my worldly cares, fears, anxieties disappear, and are of as little significance as a puff of wind. In prayer my soul inwardly exults with lively thoughts at what Thou art doing for Thy church. . . . In prayer I am lifted above the frowns and flatteries of life, and taste heavenly joys; entering into the eternal world I can give myself to Thee with all my heart, to be Thine for ever. In prayer I can place all my concerns in Thy hands, to be entirely at Thy disposal, having no will or interest of my own. In prayer I can intercede for my friends, ministers, sinners, the church, Thy kingdom to come, with greatest freedom, ardent hopes, as a son to his father.[3]

Anxious? Go to your Lord in prayer. And while you are praying, remember that the Holy Spirit and Jesus are praying for you at the same time (Romans 8:26–27, 34).

> Cast your cares on the Lord and he will sustain you; he will never let the righteous be shaken (Psalm 55:22; NIV).

Now that is an offer we shouldn't refuse.

The Cure for Care

J.R. Miller

There is no lesson that is urged more continuously or more earnestly in the Scriptures than that a Christian should never worry or let care oppress his heart. He is to live without distraction and with peace unbroken even in the midst of the most trying experiences.

If, then, we are never to be anxious, never to take distracting thought, what are we to do with the thousand things calculated to perplex us and produce anxiety? If we are not to take thought about these matters, who will do it for us? Who is to think for us? Who is to unravel the tangles for our unskilled fingers? When cares and anxieties come to our hearts, what are we to do with them?

3. https://www.goodreads.com/author/quotes/14002607.The_Valley_of_Vision.

It was a saying of Luther that we cannot prevent the birds flying about our heads, but we can prevent them building their nests in our hair. In like manner, it is impossible to keep cares from flocking in great swarms around us, but it is our own fault if they are allowed to make nests in our hearts.

We are apt to say, "Oh yes, but my trial is peculiar. It is one of those that cannot be kept out, laid down or cast off." But there is no such exception made in the divine plan of living marked out for us in the inspired word. Nothing, small or great, is to disturb our peace. We may have sorrow or suffering or toil or painful stress and strain — but never worry. What, then, is the divine life-plan? What are we to do with our cares?

We are to bring the matter as literally to Him as we would carry a broken watch to the watchmaker's, leaving it for him to repair and readjust. A little child playing with a handful of cords, when they begin to get into a tangle, goes at once to her mother, that her patient fingers may unravel the snarl. May not many of us learn a lesson from the little child? Would it not be better for us, whenever we find the slightest entanglement in any of our affairs, or the arising of any perplexity, to take it at once to God, that His skillful hands may set it right? Then, having taken it to Him, and put it into His hands, we are to leave it with Him; having gotten it off our own shoulder upon His, we are to allow it to remain there.

But it is just at this point that most of us fail. We pray about our cares, but do not cast them off. We make supplication, but do not unload our burdens. Praying does us no good. It makes us no more contented, or submissive, or patient, or peaceful. We do not get the worries out of our own hands at all. This is the vital point in the whole matter.

We are to commit our way to the Lord, trust Him and be at peace. The only thing that concerns us is our duty. God will weave the web into patterns of beauty unless by our follies and sins we mar it. But we must not hurry Him. His plans are sometimes very long, and our impatience may mar them, as well as our sins. The buds of His purposes must not be torn open. We must wait until His fingers unfold them.[4]

4. http://www.gracegems.org/Miller/cure_for_care.htm.

Chapter 16

Anxiety Reliever #12: Your God Loves You

It only seems appropriate that this is the final anxiety reliever that Jesus gave the disciples and us.

> The Father Himself **loves you,** because you have loved Me and have believed that I came forth from the Father (John 16:27).

Anxiety reliever number 12: God loves you. He loves you more than you will ever grasp.

> For this reason I bow my knees before the Father, from whom every family in heaven and on earth derives its name, that He would grant you, according to the riches of His glory, to be strengthened with power through His Spirit in the inner man, so that Christ may dwell in your hearts through faith; and that you, being rooted and grounded in love, may be able to comprehend with all the saints what is the **breadth** and **length** and **height** and **depth**, and to know the love of Christ which **surpasses knowledge**, that you may be filled up to all the fullness of God (Ephesians 3:14–19).

In order to begin to grasp the breadth and depth of God's love for us, His love needs to be understood biblically. If we fail to grasp **why**, **how,** and **who** God loves, anxiety reliever 12 will not only be worthless, but detrimental to us.

On the other hand, if you can comprehend God's love correctly, this anxiety reliever will not only reduce your anxiety, it will grow you immensely in your love for God. Be warned, this is not as easy as it sounds and, sadly, most Christians never grasp this.

Why Does God Love Us?

Do you know why God loves you? Because that is the way He is (1 John 4:7–8). In a sense, He can't help it. It is His nature (Psalm 86:15). He bleeds love. God loves us because He loves us.

> By this the **love of God** was manifested in us, that God has sent His only begotten Son into the world so that we might live through him. In **this is love**, not that we loved God, but that **he loved us** and sent his Son to be the **propitiation** for our sins. Beloved, if **God so loved us**, we also ought to love one another (1 John 4:9–11).

> I have been crucified with Christ and I no longer live, but Christ lives in me. The life I now live in the body, I live by faith in the Son of God, who **loved me** and **gave Himself for me** (Galatians 2:20).

God actually loved us *before* He sent His Son to die for us.

> For **God so loved** the world that he gave his only Son, that whoever believes in him should not perish but have eternal life (John 3:16; ESV).

> But God demonstrates **His own love** toward us, in that while we were yet **sinners**, Christ died for us (Romans 5:8).

Don't miss that. God loved us before He sent Jesus to reconcile us to Himself. It is His love that motivated Him to rescue rebels. He continues to show that love to sinners every day as He pours out blessing upon blessing even for the wicked (Matthew 5:45).

God is so loving that He actually loves people who are still in Adam. He doesn't merely tolerate them, He loves wicked, unregenerate sinners. God provides air, water, health, rain, cars, homes, jobs, and money to billions of rebels every day. Who does such a thing? Only God. Why does He do such a thing? Because that is the way He is.

How long would you provide for a dog that nipped your fingers every time you tried to pet or feed him? Yet God lavishes love and goodness on those who are far worse than a rabid dog.

God loves Christians in a special way because we are in His Son, but God also loves Muslims, Mormons, Hindus, Buddhists, cult members, and atheists. God loves false converts, heretics, and even those who persecute Christians. God loves socialists, communists, fascists, and greedy capitalists. God loves the self-righteous. God loves swingers. God loves convicts. God loves the world, because He is love.

To be certain, God is more than love, but the fact that love is one of His most glorious attributes is undeniable. God loves because He is love.

How Does God Love Us?

God's love is not a sentimental love. It isn't ooey gooey, and it certainly is not a romantic love for us.

God's love is not a quid pro quo love. God loves lavishly without expectation of reciprocity.

God's love is not based on the object of His affection. God's love is an agape love; a self-sacrificing love based on His character and not on our behavior or value.

God's love is not in response to our love for Him. God always loves first.

God's love is not preferential. God does not only love princes; He also loves paupers (Job 34:19). God doesn't play favorites.

God is the epitome and embodiment of agape love, and you and I are the fortunate recipients of His sacrificial love.

God doesn't have to warm up to people in order to love them. God doesn't ever need to recharge His love batteries by taking a break from people. God doesn't ever waver, even a little, in His love for humans.

Who Does God Love?

If you can strap in for this bumpy ride, you will come out on the other side with a more profound understanding of the potency of God's love for you.

Contrary to the secular self-esteem movement and far too many evangelicals, God does not love you because you are loveable. One of America's most popular pastors gushes, "If God had a refrigerator, He would have your picture on it." Wrong. God has a picture of us, but it is not on His fridge. It is on a Wanted poster.

Because of Adam, we are born into sin and we spend our lives sinning. We are not sinners because we sin; we sin because we are sinners. Our very natures are in bondage to sin (Romans 6:20) and we are totally depraved (Romans 8:6–8; Ephesians 2:1–5; John 8:34). That does not mean we have no capacity for good, but it does mean all of our members, functions, and thoughts are corrupted and bent toward evil.

> Behold, I was brought forth in iniquity, and **in sin** my mother conceived me (Psalm 51:5).

> The wicked are estranged **from the womb**; these who speak lies go astray **from birth** (Psalm 58:3).

Not only are we born sinners, we are born with our tiny little baby fingers wrapped in a fist — a fist we perpetually shake at God because, by nature, we hate Him.

> Because the mind set on the flesh is **hostile toward God**; for it does not subject itself to the law of God, for it is not even able to do so, and those who are in the flesh cannot please God (Romans 8:7–8).

> Jesus answered them, "Truly, truly, I say to you, everyone who commits sin is the **slave of sin**" (John 8:34).

God's love would be impressive if He loved:

- Non-sinful human beings
- Sort of sinful human beings
- Very sinful human beings

God does not love those people because those people don't exist. Instead, God loves totally, thoroughly, and completely depraved, diabolical, degenerate, debauched, dishonest, decadent, dissolute, dissipated wretches (yes, I did use a thesaurus for all of the "d" words that describe us).

Because of the Fall, you and I struggle to see ourselves like that. Because I love myself so much, I lack the ability to see myself as I actually am.

- Am I so loveable that God can't help but love me?
- Am I so amazing that God found me simply irresistible?
- Am I so handsome, pretty, rich, smart, wise, witty, athletic (or a thousand other things) that God longed to be in a relationship with me?

Our fallen nature tends to think so. Because of the Fall, we love ourselves profoundly and hate God intensely. How do I know? Jesus tells me so.

> Jesus answered "... YOU SHALL LOVE THE LORD YOUR GOD WITH ALL YOUR HEART, AND WITH ALL YOUR SOUL, AND WITH ALL YOUR MIND, AND WITH ALL YOUR STRENGTH.' The second is this, 'YOU SHALL **LOVE YOUR NEIGHBOR AS YOURSELF**.' There is no other commandment greater than these" (Mark 12:29–31).

Most secular and evangelical counselors encourage us to just love ourselves. Jesus' words fly right into the face of that advice. We love ourselves so much that Jesus uses our love for self as the highest standard of human love. Delighting in ourselves is wrong for two reasons:

1. God should be our supreme love, not us
2. We aren't worthy of that kind of love

Because of our profound love of all things us, we do not see ourselves in truth. We need an external tool to see what we are really like. We need a mirror to see our true reflection. God has graciously provided that mirror; it is called the Law of God. These laws are a perfect reflection of Himself (Romans 2:19). His laws, which reflect His character and nature, are the standard by which He judges us.

God does not compare us to others, like Hitler, He compares us to Himself. God sees us through the prism of absolute holiness and perfection as reflected in His moral laws. These laws are designed to show us how wonderful we really aren't (Romans 7:7). When we use the law of God as a mirror to hold it up to ourselves, we see our true selves. And the image is not very pretty.

If you can bear the sight, let's put that mirror in front of your face for a moment. What you are going to see is, frankly, ugly. But once you see yourself in truth, then and only then will you stand in awe of God's love for you.

God **loves** perfectly: do you? Do you love each and every person on the planet with a completely self-sacrificing love? God does. Do you meet His standard? Do you even love your family that way, every minute of every day? Me neither.

God does not meet the standard of truth, He is **truth**. Everything He says, does, and thinks is true. Has every word that has proceeded out of your mouth always been true? Have you always been perfectly precise and never shady with every single word? Me neither.

God is **pure**; He never thinks a dirty thought. Have you always maintained perfect purity in thought, word and deed? Me neither.

God is perfectly **kind**. Have you ever been snarky, bitter, sarcastic, mean, or hateful in speech toward another image bearer of God? Have you always used your words to edify and not tear down? Me neither.

God **loves** Himself more than anything in the universe. The Father, Son, and Holy Spirit are in perfect unity and love each other perfectly. Do you love God like that? Do you love Him with all of your heart, soul, mind, and strength? Is your day spent in praise of the greatest being in the solar system? Me neither.

The Bible is right when it says we have all gone astray (Isaiah 53:6). The Bible is right when it calls us helpless, ungodly sinners who are enemies of God and slaves to sin (Romans 5:6, 8, 10).

The Law reveals that you and I are not as spanky as we think.

> There is **none** righteous, not even one;
> There is **none** who understands,
> There is **none** who seeks for God;
> **All** have turned aside, together they have become useless;
> There is **none** who does good,
> There is **not even one**.
> Their throat is an **open grave**,
> With their tongues they keep **deceiving**,
> The **poison** of asps is under their lips;
> Whose mouth is full of **cursing** and **bitterness**;
> Their feet are swift to shed blood,
> Destruction and misery are in their paths,
> And the path of peace they have not known.
> There is no fear of God before their eyes (Romans 3:10–18).

Not only does the Bible describe our sin as the stench of an open grave (Romans 5:13), it says our sin is like dog vomit (Proverbs 26:11), the oozing puss of an open sore (1 Kings 8:37–38), leprosy (Leviticus 13), the venom of snakes (Romans 3:13) and even like a woman's used menstrual cloth (Isaiah 64:6). Our sin is beyond filthy. Dirt isn't as dirty as we are.

That is what God sees when He looks at us. That news should totally demolish our self-esteem. We are unlovable and unworthy of anything good. All of us.

None of us deserve love: we all deserve wrath. The wages of our sin is not affection from God, it is death from God (Romans 6:23).

> And you were **dead in your trespasses** and sins, in which you formerly walked according to the course of this world, according to the **prince of the power of the air**, of the spirit that is now working in the sons of disobedience. Among them we too all formerly lived in the **lusts of our flesh**, indulging the **desires of the flesh** and of the mind, and were by nature **children of wrath**, even as the rest (Ephesians 2:1–3).

Each and every one of is or was:

- Dead in our trespasses
- Lusters
- Under control of the devil
- Children of wrath

In other words, we are bad, we're bad, we're really, really bad. Left to ourselves, we would have to face an angry God on Judgment Day. Thankfully, the next verse of Ephesians 2 begins with one of the best words in the Bible: but.

> **But** God, being **rich in mercy**, because of His **great love** with which **He loved us**, even when we were **dead** in our transgressions, **made us alive** together with Christ (by grace you have been saved), and raised us up with Him, and **seated us with Him** in the heavenly places in Christ Jesus, so that in the ages to come He might show the surpassing riches of His grace in **kindness** toward us in Christ Jesus (Ephesians 2:4–7).

Even though we hated God, He not only loved us, He loved us enough to send His only Son to die for us (1 John 4:10). Not only did He send His Son to take the punishment we deserve for our rebellion, but He is going to resurrect us to new life. Not only is He going to resurrect us, He will seat us with Him in the heavenly places (Ephesians 2:6).

If that doesn't make you want to sing "Amazing love, how can it be? That Thou my God, would die for me?" then nothing will.

God should utterly crush, demolish, and destroy vile, wretched sinners. Instead, God lavishes His love on vile, wretched sinners.

> For while we were still **helpless**, at the right time Christ died for the **ungodly**. For one will hardly die for a righteous man; though perhaps for the good man someone would dare even to die. But God demonstrates **His own love** toward us, in that while we were **yet sinners**, Christ died for us. **Much more** then, having now been justified by His blood, we shall be saved from the wrath of God through Him. For if while we were **enemies** we were reconciled to God through the death of His Son, **much more**, having been reconciled, we shall be saved by His life. And **not only this**, but we also exult in God through our Lord Jesus Christ, through whom we have now received the reconciliation (Romans 5:6–11).

You and I are inclined to love people and pets that are loveable, but we want nothing to do with jerks and rabid animals. But God does. God loves sinners. God loves the worst of the worst. God's love is so great that He loves perverts, Wall Street criminals, rapists, murderers, liars, thieves, child molesters, homosexuals, drug dealers, us.

> In this is love, not that we loved God, but that **He loved us** and sent His Son to be the propitiation for our sins (1 John 4:10).

God's love for us is knee-bending good news; that the King of kings and Lord of lords would stoop to not only love, but die, for rebels. Does God love you? Of course He does — He sent His Son to die for you. But He loves you despite yourself, not because of yourself. That perspective crushes our self-love and elevates His love for us. It also makes His love beyond anything we could think or imagine.

What a shame that people miss out on the profound nature of God's love. What a shame that too many counselors point our affections toward something puny by telling us to "just love yourself more."

The problem with telling ourselves to just "love myself more," is threefold.

1. We know in our hearts that we just aren't that loveable. We know our thoughts and the deeds we have done in darkness that no other

human knows about. We know what we are really like on the inside and it truly isn't pretty.

2. God tells us to love Him supremely, not ourselves.
3. It just doesn't work. No matter how hard some of us try to feel better about the sins of our past and our anxieties about tomorrow, loving ourselves just doesn't seem to get the job done.

The Bible offers a more sound, profound, and biblical observation: you and I are NOT loveable, but God loves us anyway. We must swallow this pill if we are going to grasp the length, depth, and width of God's love for us.

Hard

While this news flies in the face of secularism and unbiblical Christianity, this is the news we need to find true peace. Does it sting to know that we are not all that and a bag of chips? Certainly. But consider the benefits of accepting that we are loved despite ourselves and not because of ourselves.

1. God's love for you is based on His attribute of love, not your lovable attributes. That is such a relief. If God only loves you because you are smart, funny, kind, witty, generous, pretty, handsome, in shape, or educated, then you better not lose that attribute or God won't love you anymore. The reality is, we are all going to get wrinkly, saggy, slow, and forgetful. If you believe that God loves you because "you are you," then He will not love you when you lose the attribute that makes you so loveable. Thankfully, God does not love us based on us; His love is based on Him.
2. You can rest. You don't have to maintain your wit, charm, or looks for God to love you. You are loved because He loves you, not because you perform. Whew.
3. God's love for you will last forever. No matter what your IQ is or becomes, His love endures forever (Psalm 136). No matter how creaky you become, His love endures forever. No matter how poorly you perform, His love endures forever.

If this leaves you feeling that we are not very lovable, that is excellent. We are not. But God loves you anyway! That makes His love amazing. This knowledge should astound us and leave us feeling safe and even more loved than we love ourselves.

Earthly fathers abandon their children. Spouses will grow cold toward their partner. Children can loathe their parents. God never does any of those things. God will never *not* love you. Because God is immutable and never changes (James 1:17), when He says that He is going to love you forever, He is going to love you forever. His love for you is built on His character and nature, which never changes. What a relief.

You can now wake up every morning as loved as you were when you went to bed. You can now make your way through your day, knowing that God loves you no matter what happens.

When we hear, "God loves you," we have a tendency to think, "Of course He does. I love me too." That thinking is wrong and it is the source of much anxiety. The more secure (and theologically sound) position is: I am not lovable and yet I have been shown the most radical, amazing, deep, self-sacrificing love that is eternal, unchanging, and unwavering.

God's love for you is grounded in His nature and His love for His Son. If you are in Christ, then you are as loved by the Father as Jesus Christ is. Because you are in Christ, God's love for you is constant. When do you think God loves you more?

- When you are reading porn or the Bible?
- When you are yelling at home or praising in church?
- When you are telling lies or telling the truth?
- When you are loving God or loving the world?

The answer to all of those scenarios is: NEITHER. God does NOT love you more or less based on how you are behaving, or how you are looking, or how you are thinking, or how you are acting. God loves you the same amount every single second of every single day, regardless of your performance. God's love for you is constant because His love is based on Jesus' performance and His character. When Jesus died for you, He took your rap sheet and handed you His resume. You are not just forgiven, you are seen as a citizen of the century because you receive the righteousness of Christ (2 Corinthians 5:21). Because God is love, He desired to demonstrate His mercy and loving-kindness by sending His Son to die a harsh death on a Cross (Ephesians 2:7). You and I are the unworthy recipients of this amazing grace.

The gospel is the news that devastates but ultimately elevates. The gospel says that you are so bad, God needed to die for you. The gospel also says that

God loves you so much that He did die for you. Unfathomable. Unimaginable. But not unbelievable. Believe it. Be in awe of it. Be overwhelmed by it. And let that knowledge keep you from being anxious about anything. If we fail to understand and appreciate God's love rightly, there are two inevitable consequences: fear of man and anxiety.

Fear of Man

Imagine that you are a servant in the King's castle and everyone dislikes you, but the King Himself loves you; would you care what the servants thought? Of course not. Who cares what the peasants think when the King says, "I love you, you are Mine."

Perhaps you suffer from a fear of man problem. It shows itself in so many ways:

- Insecurity
- People pleasing
- Given to gossip
- Afraid of failure
- Given to shyness
- Self-consciousness
- Easily embarrassed
- Avoidance of others
- Need to be in control
- A craving to be approved
- Reactionary and defensive
- Can't handle rejection well
- Struggle with over-sensitivity
- Overly competitive with others
- Controlled by the opinions of others[1]

These are all symptoms of the same problem — a fear of man.

> The **fear of man** brings a snare, but he who **trusts in the Lord** will be exalted (Proverbs 29:25).

Our fear of man problem snares us in many, many ways. It can make us envious, bitter, jealous, angry, afraid, self-centered, and overbearing. Fearing

1. https://rickthomas.net/synonyms-for-insecurity-or-fear-of-man/.

man can even keep us out of the game of life because we are afraid to look foolish. At its core, our fear of man problem is actually a pride problem. We want everyone to think as highly of ourselves as we do. "Fear of man" is just another term for: pride and idolatry. And we are the idol.

The antidote to your fear of man problem is to be slain and healed by understanding God's love for you. You are not lovable, but the Supreme Being of the universe loves you anyway. That knowledge will grant you both humility and joy. As you grow in your understanding of God's love for you, a sinner, your fear of man problem will begin to disappear. Every time you find yourself fearing man, dwell on God's love for you and your fear of man problem will begin to evaporate.

Self-Love and Anxiety

Failing to recognize that we are unlovable sinners who are loved more than we can love ourselves (and that's a lot) is the cause of much of our anxiety. When we esteem ourselves highly, we are shocked, disappointed, and angry when everything in life is not the way we think it should be.

When we love ourselves supremely (and we do), then we effectively kick God to the curb and place ourselves on the throne of our lives. From that perch, we reign. We seek to fulfill the desires of our flesh and please the one we think is worthy of our praise: ourselves. When we trust and worship something less than God, hello anxiety. Idols always break the hearts of their worshipers.

Our self-love shows up in the most odious ways. There are some who are just flat out pompous; you know they love themselves by the way they walk, talk, spend, look, and brag. There are others who are subtler; they claim they are depressed because of their horrific circumstances. Why is that subtle self-love? Because this person actually thinks he deserves better treatment than what he is currently receiving.

When we pretend to be humble by moping, we are actually being proud. This is why the Bible rightly observes that "The heart is deceitful . . . and . . . wicked: who can know it?" (Jeremiah 17:9; KJV).

Anxiety is often the fruit of self-love. When you love yourself, you are only being loved by a really vile sinner. How much better to recognize that you are actually a vile sinner whom God loves? This knowledge releases you from a fear of man, destroys pride, and gives true joy and contentment.

Our fleshly tendency is to forget God's love for us and quickly downshift into self-love. That is when we must go to war. When you begin to feel anxious and unloved, you must remind yourself that God's love for you, a sinner, is far better than your love for yourself. And how should you do that? Look to the place where love was most ultimately expressed: the Cross.

Look at the Man on the tree, writhing in pain for your sake. Look at the Man on the tree, gasping for air that you might have life. Look at the Man on the tree, as His blood forms pools beneath His feet and He breathes His last breath, for you.

> What then shall we say to these things? If **God is for us**, who is against us? He who **did not spare** His own Son, but delivered Him over **for us** all, how will He not also with Him freely give us all things? Who will bring a charge against God's elect? God is the one who justifies; who is the one who condemns? Christ Jesus is He who died, yes, rather who was raised, who is at the right hand of God, who also intercedes for us. Who will separate us from the **love of Christ**? Will tribulation, or distress, or persecution, or famine, or nakedness, or peril, or sword? Just as it is written,
>
> "FOR YOUR SAKE WE ARE BEING PUT TO DEATH ALL DAY LONG; WE WERE CONSIDERED AS SHEEP TO BE SLAUGHTERED."
>
> **But** in all these things we overwhelmingly conquer through **Him who loved us**. For I am convinced that neither death, **nor** life, **nor** angels, **nor** principalities, **nor** things present, **nor** things to come, **nor** powers, **nor** height, **nor** depth, **nor** any other created thing, will be able to separate us from **the love of God**, which is in Christ Jesus our Lord (Romans 8:31–39).

Don't feel loved? It doesn't matter how you feel. The truth of the matter is, God loves you regardless of your feelings.

Are you anxious? Do you fear man? Stop and take a few decades to ponder the love that God has for you, even though you don't deserve it.

> For this reason I bow my knees before the Father, from whom every family in heaven and on earth derives its name, that He would grant you, according to the riches of His glory, to **be strengthened** with power **through His Spirit** in the inner man, so that Christ may

dwell in your hearts through faith; and that you, being rooted and **grounded in love**, may be able to comprehend with all the saints what is the **breadth** and **length** and **height** and **depth**, and to know the **love of Christ** which surpasses knowledge, that you may be filled up to all the fullness of God (Ephesians 3:14–19).

We must swallow the hard medicine that we are not lovable. But we must not stop there. We must also swallow the sweet news that God loves us anyway. That is the ultimate cure for your anxiety.

He Could Not Love You More!

Charles Spurgeon

He loved you without beginning. Before years, and centuries, and millenniums began to be counted — *your name was on His heart!* Eternal thoughts of love have been in God's bosom towards you. He has loved you without a pause; there never was a minute in which He did not love you. Your name once engraved upon His hands — has never been erased, nor will He ever blot it out of the Book of Life.

Since you have been in this world — He has loved you most patiently. You have often provoked Him; you have rebelled against Him times without number, yet He has never stayed the outflow of His heart towards you; and, blessed be His name — He never will. You are His, and you always shall be His. God's love to you is without boundary. **He could not love you more** — for He loves you like a God; and He never will love you less. All His heart belongs to you![2]

2. http://www.gracegems.org/2010/03/more.html.

Section 3:

Application

Chapter 17

Your Goal

Chances are very good that you have figured out the true intention of this book. As you have been sensing, the goal of this book has not been to make you feel better. The goal of this book has been to increase your love for God and your desire to glorify Him. The more you desire to glorify God, the more you will have joy. That is a promise directly from the mouth of the Savior.

> Just as the Father has loved Me, I have also loved you; abide in My love. If you **keep My commandments**, you will abide in My love; just as I have kept My Father's commandments and abide in His love. These things I have spoken to you so that My joy may be in you, and that **your joy** may be made full (John 15:9–11).

This book cannot bring you joy, but Jesus will bring you joy as you strive to be more and more like Him. While that formula sounds pretty easy, it is difficult for multiple reasons.

Problem #1: Our Flesh

Until our bodies are glorified, we are going to be in a perpetual battle with our sinful flesh. You have a brand-new nature (2 Corinthians 5:17), but you don't have a brand-new body. Until Jesus returns or calls you home, you are going to hear the constant siren songs of your unredeemed flesh (Romans 7).

Problem #2: Our Brains

Thanks to Adam, our brains are inclined to go dim and the result, believe it or not, is: idolatry. Instead of worshiping our Maker, we are inclined to stray after false idols.

> For even though they knew God, they did not honor Him as God or give thanks, but they became **futile in their speculations**, and their foolish heart was **darkened**. Professing to be wise, they became **fools**, and exchanged the glory of the incorruptible God for an image in the form of corruptible man and of birds and four-footed animals and crawling creatures (Romans 1:21–23).

Until you get your new brain when you get your glorified body, you are going to be in a war to keep your thinking in alignment with God's thinking. You cannot hear one sermon or read one book and be perfect.

Changing your thinking is a process and a battle. Do not fall into the trap of expecting instantaneous sanctification. It hasn't happened to anyone yet, and it isn't going to happen for you. Be comforted by that as you strive to think right. This is God's process and it is best.

PROBLEM #3: OUR FORGETFUL BRAINS

If you are feeling less anxious after reading this book, there is a reason for it. Right now, your thinking is relatively aligned with God's thinking because you have read a ton of Bible verses and biblical truth. Unfortunately, you are going to go to bed, wake up, and you will have forgotten some of the truths that you now have in your brain. As the days go by, you will forget more and more and you will progressively return to your anxious thinking. You are not a freak; this is not just common, it is universal. We all forget, all the time. Quick, what is the Pythagorean theorem you memorized in high school? See?

Forgetfulness is a major problem for us. Do not feel bad about this, you are not the only one to have this problem. Paul wrote to the Galatians and Philippian Christians to repeat what he had already taught them (Galatians 1:9).

> Further, my brothers and sisters, rejoice in the Lord! It is no trouble for me to write the **same things** to you **again**, and it is a safeguard for you (Philippians 3:1; NIV).

Both Peter and Jude (Jude 1:5) found it necessary to repeat the basic truths of the faith.

> Therefore, I will always be ready to **remind you** of these things, even though you **already know them**, and have been established in the truth which is present with you (2 Peter 1:12).

You do not forget biblical truths because you are dumb or a bad Christian. You forget because of the noetic affects of the Fall. Our brains fail to think correctly and remember the biblical truths that get our thinking back on track. That is a recipe for disaster. That is the bad news.

The good news is that God can and will fix our thinking. But He is not going to do it without our participation. This is not an option for us, this is a command:

> And do not be conformed to this world, but **be transformed** by the **renewing of your mind**, so that you may prove what the will of God is, that which is good and acceptable and perfect (Romans 12:2).

The recipe for peace is simple: think like God and you will feel less anxious. Paul explains this for us:

> Do not lie to one another, since you laid aside the old self with its evil practices, and have put on the **new self who is being renewed to a true knowledge** according to the **image of the One** who created him — a renewal in which there is no distinction between Greek and Jew, circumcised and uncircumcised, barbarian, Scythian, slave and freeman, but Christ is all, and in all (Colossians 3:9–11).

The gospel screams reconciliation, but it also hollers restoration. God saves us to reconcile us to Himself, but He does not leave us in our broken, fallen state. He immediately goes about the business of reversing the effects of the Fall so we think, act, and feel like He does. Now that God has forgiven you through Jesus, He wants to progressively fix you to look like Jesus.

How does He do that? Colossians 3:10 makes it clear: through true knowledge. And where do we find that true knowledge? There is only one place: the Bible.

> So Jesus was saying to those Jews who had believed Him, "If you continue in **My word**, then you are truly disciples of Mine; and you will know the truth, and the truth will **make you free**" (John 8:31–32).

This is the order of things:

1. You and I are dead in our trespasses and sins (Ephesians 2:1).
2. Our brains could not understand spiritual things (1 Corinthians 2:14).
3. God's Holy Spirit regenerated us (Titus 3:5).
4. We repent and trust Jesus (Mark 1:15).
5. God forgives us of all of our sins — past, present, and future (Colossians 2:14).
6. God progressively sanctifies us by fixing our thinking through the means He has provided us.
7. We do the good works He has assigned us to do (Titus 3:5–8).

> For we also once were **foolish** ourselves, **disobedient**, **deceived**, **enslaved** to various **lusts** and **pleasures**, spending our life in **malice** and **envy**, hateful, **hating** one another. But when the kindness of God our Savior and **His love** for mankind appeared, He **saved us**, not on the basis of deeds which we have done in righteousness, but according to **His mercy**, by the washing of **regeneration** and renewing by the **Holy Spirit**, whom He poured out upon us richly through Jesus Christ our Savior, so that being **justified** by His grace we would be made heirs according to the hope of eternal life. This is a trustworthy statement; and concerning these things I want you to speak confidently, so that those who have believed God will be careful to engage in **good deeds**. These things are good and profitable for men (Titus 3:3–8).

The solution to our anxiety (and all emotional issues) is very simple: get saved, read our Bibles, and work with God's Holy Spirit to transform our thinking, which will fix our emotions and produce fruit of obedience. This is the Christian life.

After Jesus gave the disciples 12 anxiety relievers, He stopped to pray on His way to the Garden of Gethsemane. He first prayed for Himself, and then He prayed for the disciples and for us! Let's eavesdrop on this amazing glimpse into the relationship between the Father and the Son.

> But now I come to You; and these things I speak in the world so that they may **have My joy** made full in themselves (John 17:13).

Once again, gentle Jesus prayed *for* us that we might have joy. Do not miss this staggering juxtaposition. Jesus is facing the wrath of the Father for the sins of His disciples and us, and He petitions the Father for our joy. Did you forget that Jesus is for you? Jesus prayed,

> **Sanctify them** in the truth; Your **word is truth** (John 17:17).

Jesus then prayed that we will be a sanctified (holy) people. Jesus wants us to be holy; He does not want us to be moral. There is an eternal difference between those two words. Morality is mere external conformity to a list of do's and don'ts. Holiness is an internal orientation that affects the will, mind, emotions, conscience, everything. To be moral is to force oneself to behave. Holiness is an internal desire to be pleasing to the One who saved us.

And how exactly does Jesus prescribe our holiness? Take a look at John 17:17 again.

> **Sanctify them** in the truth; Your **word is truth** (John 17:17).

There it is again! The ordained means for our sanctification is the Word. Notice how Jesus describes the Word; He says that the Word is truth. And who is the truth? Jesus had just told the disciples that He is the way, the truth, and the life (John 14:6). Additionally, the first words of John's Gospel are, "In the beginning was the Word." And who was the Word? Jesus. The Word of truth reveals Jesus Christ.

In order to be sanctified, we need to study the Word about Jesus. That means we need to read the Bible with a focus on Him. We need to read the Old Testament, understanding that it is pointing to Jesus in the New Testament. We need to read the New Testament with a Cross-centered perspective and an eye on the return of Jesus. When we do that, we will become increasingly sanctified as He transforms our minds through His Word and the power of the Holy Spirit.

That sounds so simple, but the problem is that we read and forget, we read and forget. That is why Jesus commands us to continue in His Word. Because of our forgetful noodles, we have to constantly be in the Word.

Thankfully, God has provided many ways for us to digest His Word: these are called the means of grace. These means do not forgive us of our sins (Jesus did that), but they grow us in our faith through knowledge of Him.

If we want our anxiety to go away, then we must constantly partake of these means of grace that focus on Jesus. If we fail to partake of these means, then we can plan on not growing in holiness and thus, struggling with anxiety until we die. But if we partake of these FIVE means of grace, then we will progressively start to think like God. And God isn't anxious.

MEANS #1: THE WORD

In the Book of Acts, we see the five means of grace as we see how the early church spent their time.

> So then, those who had **received his word** were baptized; and that day there were added about three thousand souls. They were continually devoting themselves to the **apostles' teaching** (Acts 2:41–42).

Unbelievers heard the Word preached, got saved, got baptized, and devoured the teaching of the Apostles. If you want your thinking, and hence, your emotions fixed, devote yourself to the Word.

- Listen to sermons from faithful preachers
- Attend Bible studies
- Read your Bible every day

A failure to have a customized, consistent reading plan is downright perilous (1 Thessalonians 2:13).

> Anyone who runs ahead and **does not continue** in the teaching of Christ does not have God; whoever continues in **the teaching** has both the Father and the Son (2 John 1:9; NIV).

How do we abide in the teaching? By continuously studying it so we don't forget it. Jesus reiterates this in John 15.

> **Abide** in Me, and I in you. As the branch cannot bear fruit of itself unless it abides in the vine, so neither can you unless you abide in Me. I am the vine, you are the branches; he who abides in Me and I in him, he **bears much fruit**, for apart from Me you can do nothing. If anyone does not abide in Me, he is **thrown away** as a branch and dries up; and they gather them, and cast them into the fire and they are burned. If you abide in Me, and **My words abide in you**, ask whatever you wish, and it will be done for you (John 15:4–7).

We abide in His Word when we continually digest it so we don't forget it. You can digest the Word by reading it or listening to sermons about it. This requires diligence, faithfulness, and effort. Salvation is monergistic (God alone saves), but sanctification is synergistic (we work with the Holy Spirit, who gives us the ability to obey).

Reading the Bible means more than just skimming through it. We must interpret it, digest it, apply it, and be transformed by it. When we listen to a sermon, we are to hear it, ponder it, and let it stir and affect us.

If you have been consuming the Word but it has not been affecting your thinking and emotions, then something is wrong. There are several potential reasons for this:

- You are sitting under bad teaching
- You are not understanding what you read
- You are actually learning, but you do not fully trust the Word
- You amass knowledge, but you do not submit to what you learn

Knowledge without transformation is worthless. If the Word is not changing you, then you need to change the way you are consuming it. The Word must go from our eyes and ears to our brains and down to our hearts.

Memorize the Word

Psalm 119:1 gives us the formula for not sinning: hiding God's Word in our hearts. To be sanctified is to consume and memorize the Word. If you do nothing but memorize Bible verses that speak to your anxiety, you will be light years ahead of most Christians. There are countless Christians who struggled with anxiety and panic attacks who memorized anti-anxiety verses and waved goodbye to their panic attacks and hyperventilating. Memorizing God's Word works.

Here are some verses to get you started.

> Do not fear, for I am with you; do not anxiously look about you, for I am your God. I will strengthen you, surely I will help you, surely I will uphold you with My righteous right hand (Isaiah 41:10).

> Commit your way to the Lord, trust also in Him, and He will do it (Psalm 37:5).

> Look at the birds of the air that they do not sow, nor reap nor gather into barns, and yet your heavenly Father feeds them. Are you not worth much more than they (Matthew 6:26)?

> So we can confidently say, "The Lord is my helper; I will not fear; what can man do to me?" (Hebrews 13:6; ESV).
>
> And my God will supply every need of yours according to his riches in glory in Christ Jesus (Philippians 4:19; ESV).
>
> For this light momentary affliction is preparing for us an eternal weight of glory beyond all comparison (2 Corinthians 4:17; ESV).
>
> He will wipe away every tear from their eyes, and death shall be no more, neither shall there be mourning, nor crying, nor pain anymore, for the former things have passed away (Revelation 21:4).

If you don't care for these, just search through your Bible for verses that remove fear when you ponder them. There are thousands to choose from!

MEANS #2: FELLOWSHIP WITH OTHER CHRISTIANS

God provides another way for us to consume the Word: fellowship.

> They were continually devoting themselves to the apostles' teaching and **to fellowship** (Acts 2:42).

The second means of grace is fellowship with other like-minded Christians. God uses other Christians to help us understand the Word better. Christian fellowship is not watching a football game with fellow Christians. Fellowship is not having a salad and a chat with a girlfriend for lunch. True Christian fellowship is spending time with other believers talking about the Word.

When you and I spend time with other believers talking about what God has been teaching us through His Word, then we are merely consuming His Word through a different vehicle. The best place to do this is the local church. The early believers gathered together and practiced their Christian walk together. There is only one way to do the "one anothers" of Scripture: by being together.

- We can't counsel one another if we never see one another (Romans 15:14).
- We can't love one another if we don't fellowship with one another (John 15:17).
- We can't build up one another if we don't spend time with one another (Romans 14:19).

- We can't bear one another's burdens if we don't interact with one another (Galatians 6:2).
- We can't speak truth (Ephesians 4:25) or be kind to one another (Ephesians 4:32) if we never see one another.

Christianity is most certainly an individualistic religion, but it is also a family affair. The local church is the ideal place to gather with your family and encourage one another.

> Let the **word of Christ** richly dwell within you, with all wisdom teaching and admonishing **one another** with **psalms** and **hymns** and **spiritual songs**, singing with thankfulness in your hearts to God (Colossians 3:16).

God's ordained means for consuming the means of grace is the local church. So find the best local church you can, join it, fellowship, and watch your anxiety disappear.

Means #3 and #4: The Ordinances

Another great way to consume the Word is participating in the ordinances of the church.

> They were continually devoting themselves to the apostles' teaching and to fellowship, to the **breaking of bread** . . . (Acts 2:42).

The new believers got saved, baptized, and then they regularly participated in the Lord's Supper (breaking of bread). When we watch someone get baptized, we hear and see the gospel. Baptism is a picture of the death, burial, and Resurrection of Jesus. Baptism is also a symbolic picture of salvation as someone re-enacts their death to self, cleansing and being raised to new life in Christ.

> Do you not know that all of us who have been baptized into Christ Jesus were **baptized into His death**? We were buried therefore with Him by baptism into death, in order that, **just as** Christ was raised from the dead by the glory of the Father, we too might walk in newness of life (Romans 6:3–4).

When we participate in the Lord's Supper we are being physically reminded that Jesus' body was broken and His blood was shed for the forgiveness of our sins. The Lord's Supper is a picture of the gospel. When we think deeply about the gospel by partaking of the Lord's Supper, then we get spiritually fed.

> The Lord Jesus in the night in which He was betrayed took bread; and when He had given thanks, He broke it and said, "This is My body which is for you; do this **in remembrance** of Me." In the same way He took the cup also after supper, saying, "This cup is the new covenant in My blood; do this, as often as you drink it, **in remembrance** of Me." For as often as you eat this bread and drink the cup, you **proclaim the Lord's death** until He comes (1 Corinthians 11:23–26).

Neither the Lord's Supper nor baptisms have mystical properties that forgive or sanctify you. Their power lies in the truth that they preach. The sacraments grow you because the sacraments preach the Word.

Means #5: Prayer

It would make sense that prayer is the final means of grace because Jesus already told us that we are to ask God for anything through prayer (John 14:13). They were continually devoting themselves to the apostles' teaching and to fellowship, to the breaking of bread and **to prayer** (Acts 2:42).

Prayer helps our anxiety in two ways:

1. We communicate our cares and needs to God knowing that He cares for us (1 Peter 5:7). It is a relief to be able to unload all of our burdens on the One who cares, and carries and cures our problems.
2. We are to pray "in Jesus' name," which is another way of staying in alignment with His Word. When we organize our prayers around God's Word, we are fed by the Word of truth.

When you begin to feel anxious, cast all of your cares on God through prayer and watch how He removes your anxiety.

> I sought the Lord, and He answered me, and **delivered me** from all my fears (Psalm 34:4).

A walk in the woods can be therapeutic, but the means of grace are God's ordained means for helping you. The more you partake of these means of grace, the less anxious you will be.

The Great Physician has diagnosed your anxious emotions as a faith and thinking problem. He has given you the prescription to progressively make you think and feel better: His Word. The more you consume the Word, the more you will look like Jesus. The sooner you start, the sooner you will have peace.

Be Ever Looking unto Jesus!

George Everard, 1884

"Beloved, now we are children of God, and it has not appeared as yet what we will be. We know that when He appears, *we will be like Him*, because *we will see Him just as He is!* And everyone who has this hope *fixed* on Him purifies himself, just as He is pure" 1 John 3:2–3.

Note the transforming power of this sight. There will be a perfect conformity to Christ's image. Sin will be annihilated in the soul, and no temptation ever be able to stir one thought of evil. This mortal body will put on its garments of glory and immortality. In heavenly purity, in unwearied brightness and activity, in an atmosphere of love, born of the love that inflames the heart of Christ — the risen saint will be *satisfied* as he awakes in the likeness of His Savior! And with the sight of Christ Himself, there will be ten thousand sights that will indefinitely multiply the Christian's joy. What will it be to behold angel and archangel, cherubim and seraphim — and all doing homage to Him whom we love!

What will be the sight of that *celestial city* pictured to us in the Revelation in such glowing words — but whose true glory and beauty no heart of mortal man has ever yet conceived?

Christian, rejoice! *This sight is for you!* This hope is for you! Unworthy in your own eyes; oft lamenting your own infirmities, your lack of love, your failings in the Master's service — yet your *eyes* shall see and your *heart* shall overflow with the eternal joys which are at God's right hand.

Nay, let your eye be upward, seeking daily aid and grace from above. **Be ever looking unto Jesus** as your great Pattern and Exemplar, and also as the Fountain-head of all supplies of wisdom, strength, and consolation!

"Let us also lay aside every encumbrance and the sin which so easily entangles us, and let us run with endurance the race that is set before us, *fixing our eyes on Jesus,* the author and perfecter of faith!" Hebrews 12:1–2.[1]

1. http://www.gracegems.org/2015/12/looking.html.

Chapter 18

Your Plan

Let's get started on the path of peace.

Jesus said,

> "If you **know** these things, you are **blessed** if you **do** them" (John 13:17).

Jesus promises that when we know the things of God and actually do them, the result will be peace (blessing). This is precisely what the Westminster Catechism stated when it answered the question, "What is the chief end of man?" The answer it gives is: "The chief end of man is to glorify God and enjoy Him forever."

Knowing God is the highest endeavor in the world. As we get to know God, we are enjoying the most enjoyable thing in the universe. When we pursue anything else, we will ultimately be unhappy because we are not living the way we were designed to live.

If a man works at McDonalds but spends his time at work trying to build an airplane, he is going to be a very unhappy and frustrated employee. That is true for us too. We were designed to know God and enjoy Him forever. Any other pursuit will leave us in the pits. That is precisely what the wisest man in the world concluded.

King Solomon wrote what appears to be the most depressing book ever, Ecclesiastes. For 12 chapters, he laments that everything in life is meaningless. Knowledge and labor is meaningless. Wealth and property is worthless. Fame and fortune is meaningless. If it weren't for the last two verses of the book, Ecclesiastes would depress a hyena. Thankfully, Solomon puts our entire existence into correct perspective with two sentences.

> The conclusion, when all has been heard, is: **fear God** and **keep His commandments**, because this applies to every person. For God will bring every act to judgment, everything which is hidden, whether it is good or evil (Ecclesiastes 12:13–14).

Whew! There is a reason to live. When we live for God, then, and only then, are we living rightly and purposefully. When our chief goal is to glorify God and enjoy Him forever, then everything else in life is sweet. When God is at the center, then everything in our orbit makes sense. The battle for the Christian is to keep God there.

So let's get started on a plan to live the best possible life by creating a plan to remove the idols of our lives and let God sit squarely on the throne of our lives.

Step One: Re-orient Your Trust

The world and our unredeemed flesh screams, "Trust me." The Bible shouts, "No, trust me." It is time for you to determine whom you are going to obey. The Christian life is a sold-out life (Matthew 12:30). We cannot have our feet in two different kingdoms. If you keep one foot in the world and one foot in the Word, then the Bible has a word to describe you: double-minded.

> A double minded man is unstable in **all** his ways (James 1:8; KJV).

Ouch. Not only does the Bible tag us, it also explains why our emotions are wobbly. Double-mindedness, or a lack of total commitment to God, makes us unstable. If our affections and trust have been half-hearted, that is the source of our anxiety. Do you:

- Trust God and trust yourself
- Trust God and trust psychiatry
- Trust God and trust the stock market
- Trust God and trust politics and politicians

If your life is not resting squarely on the Cornerstone, Jesus Christ, then you have one foot on sinking sand. That explains why you are anxious. Cease being double-minded and you will cease being anxious.

The heavenly music is a waltz, and double-minded people dance to a different tune. They are right-handers golfing with left-handed clubs. They have their shoes on the wrong feet. They are trying to make Mongolian Beef at Chick-fil-A. You get the point.

Living for your Maker is not a downgrade; it is the ultimate upgrade (John 10:10).

> More than that, I count all things to be loss in view of the **surpassing value** of knowing Christ Jesus my Lord, for whom I have suffered the loss of all things, and **count them but rubbish** so that I may gain Christ (Philippians 3:8).

This is not a call for you to get saved, because I assume you already are. This is a call to re-orient your thinking and your life so that you are hidden in Christ, because you are (Colossians 3:3). Dedicate your life to live fully and joyfully for your King. Don't strive to live your best life now; strive to glorify your God and you will be living the abundant life, knowing that our best life is reserved for us in heaven. This is the way life was made to be lived. If you skip this step, you will continue to struggle with anxiety.

Determine now that you are casting your lot with Jesus. Determine that you are "all in." Surrender totally, completely, willingly. You are building your life on something; why would you not commit to building it on the One who created and sustains the universe?

Why not settle this once and for all? Why not totally surrender your will to the One who died for you? Why delay? Determine like Joshua that you are all in. Joshua said,

> If it is disagreeable in your sight to serve the Lord, choose for yourselves today whom you will serve: whether the gods which your fathers served which were beyond the River, or the gods of the Amorites in whose land you are living; but as for me and my house, **we will serve the Lord** (Joshua 24:15).

Let it be said of you when you die, "This is one whose life was built on the foundation of God and His Word." When you do, you will read God's Word and it will come alive to you and you will be blessed in ways that you cannot begin to imagine.

> Trust in the Lord with **all your heart**
> And **do not lean** on your own understanding.

In all your ways acknowledge Him,
And He will make your paths straight.
Do not be wise in **your own eyes**;
Fear the Lord and turn away from evil.
It will be **healing** to your body
And **refreshment** to your bones (Proverbs 3:5–8).

God wants to make your emotional paths straight. God wants to heal your thinking. But there is a string attached!

- God will make your paths straight . . . if you trust Him fully.
- God will still your soul . . . if you trust in Him with all your heart.
- God will calm your troubled heart . . . if you do not lean on your own understanding.

God helps those who do *not* help themselves; but He does help those who trust completely in Him. Humble yourself by trusting fully in Him and He will be your comfort, peace, strength, hope, joy, everything.

- Surrender totally this day to your Master and He will be your peace as you read His Word.
- Surrender completely this day to your Lord and He will heal your troubled emotions as you continue in His Word.
- Surrender to Jesus and your sympathetic High Priest will apply balm to your wounded heart as you study Him in His Word.
- Surrender to Jesus, the Prince of Peace, and you will have His peace as you study Him in His Word.
- Surrender to Jesus. Study Jesus. Look at Jesus in His Word, and you will actually become like Him.

If you need to, take a few moments to talk to your God and surrender.

Step Two: Change Your Language

The world would like to persuade us that anxiety is a disease. The Bible should persuade you that anxiety is a sin. That should give you hope! You do not have a mental disorder, you simply have a sin problem. When we reject worldly labels and use biblical language, then the Bible will help us with it.

This simple step might help you to resist the temptation to worry. The next time you are inclined to be anxious about the future, remember that you are about to sin. Then remember that Jesus had to die for sins. See if that doesn't motivate you to not be anxious.

Step Three: Repent

If you have never repented of your sinful anxiety, then now is the time. Tell your God that you are sorry for lacking faith. Apologize for trusting yourself. Repent of making yourself an idol.

> If we say that we have no sin, we are deceiving ourselves and the truth is not in us. If we **confess** our sins, He is faithful and righteous to **forgive** us our sins and to **cleanse** us from all unrighteousness. If we say that we have not sinned, we make Him a liar and His word is not in us (1 John 1:8–10).

Join the rest of us by confessing your sin of self-righteousness to the One who is faithful and just to forgive you and cleanse you. Don't wait for God to humble you; you don't want that. Humble yourself and He will begin exalting you (James 4:7).

Step Four: Mortify, Mortify, Mortify

Your life is no longer your own. You and I are not here to please ourselves; we are here to glorify our God. The great news is, when we die to self and live for Him, then we truly live. This is a major theme in the New Testament.

> I have been **crucified with Christ**; and it is no longer I who live, but Christ lives in me; and the life which I now live in the flesh I live by faith in the Son of God, who loved me and gave Himself up for me (Galatians 2:20).

> That, in reference to your former manner of life, you lay aside the old self, which is being corrupted in accordance with the lusts of deceit, and that you be **renewed in the spirit of your mind**, and put on the new self, which in the likeness of God has been created in righteousness and holiness of the truth (Ephesians 4:22–24).

There are many, many more verses that stress death to self and new life in Christ, including Colossians 3:5; Romans 12:1; 1 Peter 4:1–2; Galatians 5:24; Romans 6:8, 11–14, 8:12–13; Galatians 6:14. All of these verses merely echo what Jesus Himself said:

> And He was saying to them all, "If anyone wishes to come after Me, he must deny himself, and **take up his cross** daily and follow Me. For whoever wishes to save his life will **lose it**, but whoever loses his life for My sake, he is the one who will **save it**" (Luke 9:23–24).

John Owen said, "Be killing sin, or it will be killing you."[1] Go to war against your anxiety. Find the strength and desire by staring at your Savior on the Cross. Read about the King who died for His servants. Study the One who demonstrated His love for you by dying for you. As you do, you will willingly and happily die to yourself.

STEP FIVE: CREATE A PLAN

If you do not create a plan for digesting the Word, you are going to get busy and distracted, and you will neglect your consumption of the Word and you will starve. Here are some ideas to get you started.

You need to create your own customized Bible reading plan by taking a look at your life to determine the schedule that works best for you. When can you find the time to read your Bible every day? If it is morning, then read your Bible with the birds. If it is evening, read the Bible with the moon. Do not adopt someone else's reading plan, create your own.

How much of the Bible should you read? As much as you want. The more you read, the more you will want to read. Get started where you are and God will bless your time in His Word.

What should you read? May I suggest you get a John MacArthur Study Bible, NASB version, and read one New Testament book at a time in any order, but read each and every footnote as you go? It may take you a while to accomplish this, but I promise, when you are done you will know more than most pastors in America.

If you are not a member of a good church where you can hear biblical sermons and enjoy Christian fellowship, find the best local church you can

1. http://www.crossroad.to/Quotes/faith/owen.htm.

and join it. Here are two sites that list reliable churches: www.tms.edu (find a pastor), or try www.9marks.org (church search).

If you want to listen to great sermons, here are some solid Bible teachers who have thousands of sermons that can be listened to for free at their websites or at www.sermonaudio.com: John MacArthur, Phil Johnson, Steve Lawson, R.C. Sproul, Art Azurdia, Alistair Begg. That should keep you busy for a while.

You will love receiving a Grace Gem every day. You have been reading them at the end of each chapter. You can subscribe for free and receive a great quote from an old dead guy every day in your inbox. Sign up at www.gracegems.org.

If you feast on the Word and apply it, you will grow. In fact, you cannot not grow if you read and heed God's Word by utilizing the means of grace.

Step Six: Prepare to Persevere

Sanctification is not an event; it is a process. You have been anxious for years, so don't expect anxiety to be eradicated overnight. Don't let that trouble you — God will be patient with you as you grow. Some days you are going to make great progress; the very next day you might fall down. This is very normal. Let God pick you up, clean you off, and set your feet back on the path. The longer you continue in His Word, the more you will have victory. Rejoice in the successes, repent of the failures, but whatever you do, don't grow weary.

Step Seven: Start Now!

Do not hesitate to start because this sounds hard. Don't be the patient who refuses treatment because it is too strenuous. Needless to say, knowing God and the pursuit of holiness is worth the effort.

Just remember that theology without the gospel quickly becomes legalism and can cause you to grow bitter and weary. Don't learn facts and laws in order to become a better person with stable emotions. Study the Word to learn more about Jesus.

Life is fleeting. Our life is a vapor (James 4:14). Don't spend it being anxious. Get started today!

> **Work out** your salvation with fear and trembling; for it is God who is **at work in you**, both to will and to work for His good pleasure (Philippians 2:12–13).

Be confident that He who began a good work in you is faithful to complete it (Philippians 1:6). God will not forsake you (Matthew 28:20). God will not leave you like an orphan to do this by yourself (John 14:18); He has given you the Comforter and His Word.

May God progressively grow you in knowledge and obedience to Him as He continually conforms you to the image of His Son as your thinking is transformed through the knowledge of His Word.

Jesus closed His words of comfort to the disciples and us by saying:

> These things I have spoken to you, so that in Me **you may have peace**. In the world you have tribulation, but take courage; I have overcome the world (John 16:33).

After He said this, He went to the Cross to die. For you.

O Wondrous Love!

James Smith, 1861

He gave Himself for us — that He might redeem us from all iniquity, and purify unto Himself a peculiar people, zealous for good works. Titus 2:14.

Note the *contrast* between the Giver — and those for whom He gave Himself.

The Giver is He who was the only begotten Son of God, the author of creation, the sustainer of the universe, the brightness of divine glory, the source and end of all things! He who was proclaimed by the prophet as "the mighty God, the everlasting Father, and the Prince of Peace." He who is declared by the apostle to be "*God* over all — blessed for evermore!"

"He gave Himself for US." For US — who at the best are *mere creatures*, between whom and our Creator, there can be no comparison. But it was not for us as *mere creatures* — but for us as base, vile, insignificant, and totally depraved creatures! We had debased ourselves, even unto Hell. Our nature could not be worse, for "the human heart is the most deceitful of all things — and desperately wicked!"

The most exalted, glorious, and holy being in the universe — gave Himself for the most vile, polluted, and degraded of His creatures! *O how astonishing!*

But He *volunteered* on our behalf, without any solicitation, offering to become our *Substitute* — to fulfill the law in our stead; our *Sacrifice* — to make a full atonement for our sins; and our Ransomer — to pay the satisfactory price for our redemption.

He engaged to bear the desert of all our sins in His own body — to suffer all that the inflexible justice of God could inflict on our Surety — and so put away our sins forever, by the sacrifice of Himself. He gave His person — for our persons; His blood — as our ransom price; and His life — for our lives.

He gave His *entire* self, doing and suffering all that was necessary to secure our release from sin's curse, and our everlasting salvation. O amazing grace of a gracious Savior!

The love of Jesus is unparalleled. Out of pure love to us who had no love to Him, nor ever would have had — but for His *first* loving us! He gave, not only His *time*, His *labor*, His *wealth* — but *Himself!* He gave His entire person as the God-man, the incarnate Jehovah!

"He gave Himself!" This was more than as if He had given *a thousand worlds* — for these He could create with a word!

"He gave Himself," and not merely to *live* for us, or *labor* for us — but even to *die* for us!

"He gave Himself," and not even to die some *easy* and honorable death — but the most painful, shameful death, that any man ever invented, or any creature ever suffered!

O wondrous love![2]

2. http://gracegems.org/Smith3/redeeming_love.htm.

OPEN & GROW

Stressed Out Small Group Kit

978-0-89221-747-2 **$49.99**

Stressed Out Leaders Guide

978-0-89221-746-5 **$11.99**

Stressed Out DVD (95 min.)

713438-10233-7 **$25.99**

Stressed Out Book

978-0-89221-743-4 **$13.99**

Includes: Leader's guide, *Stressed Out: A Practical, Biblical Approach to Anxiety* book, and DVD of practical teaching by author Todd Friel. This study is designed to be done in 5 parts lasting 60-90 minutes each and will help small groups apply Biblical truths to replace fear, anxiety, and depression with peace.

New Leaf Press
A Division of New Leaf Publishing Group
www.newleafpress.net

About the Author

Todd Friel is the host of *Wretched Radio*, a daily syndicated talk radio program, as well as host of *Wretched TV*. *Wretched Radio* is heard on 200 stations nationwide and *Wretched TV* is available in over 100 million households. Todd is the husband of one wife and father of three children.

Website: www.wretchedradio.com

Twitter: www.twitter.com/Wretchedradio

Facebook: facebookcom/wretchednetwork

Jesus Unmasked

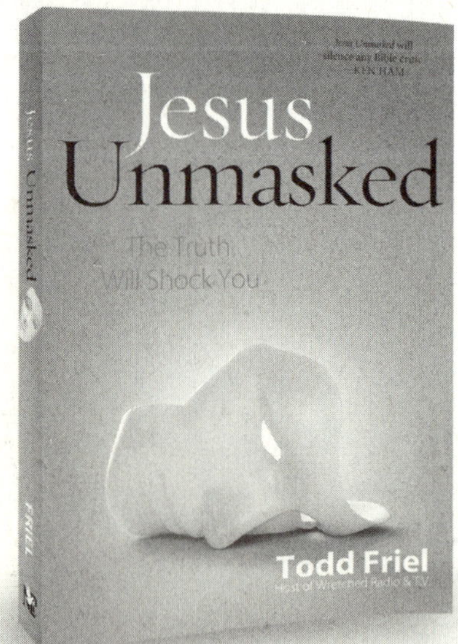

$14.99 | 978-0-89221-726-7

The Truth
Will Shock
YOU

Todd Friel
Host of Wretched Radio & T.V.

Available at NLPG.com and where fine books are sold.